THE
EVERYTHING®
JOB INTERVIEW QUESTION BOOK

Dear Reader,

Most of us could come up with a list of things we would rather do than be grilled by a prospective employer. Root canals, anyone? As a job candidate, you feel tremendous pressure to perform well because in most cases you really want the job— or at least you want the employer to offer it to you. What you may not know is that the interviewer may be feeling a bit nervous too. It is up to her to make sure the candidate she selects is a good fit for the job and for the company in general. Hiring mistakes can be costly. So, as you are sitting there wondering why she is throwing such difficult questions at you, remember that the stakes are very high . . . for everyone involved.

In the more than two decades I've spent helping people manage their careers—as the Guide to Career Planning on About .com (careerplanning.about.com) and as a job information center coordinator and career specialist in public libraries—I've heard from many people who are extremely anxious about going on job interviews. The best way to overcome the stress of job interviewing is to prepare for it as much as possible. That's why you'll find hundreds of interview questions in this book, along with great answers and ones you should avoid giving.

After reading this book you will be well prepared for your interviews. Your anxiety will be gone (mostly) and you will be able to present yourself in the best way possible.

Good luck!

Dawn Rosenberg McKay

Welcome to the EVERYTHING Series!

These handy, accessible books give you all you need to tackle a difficult project, gain a new hobby, or even brush up on something you learned back in school but have since forgotten. You can choose to read from cover to cover or just pick out information from our four useful boxes.

 Alerts

Urgent warnings

 Facts

Important snippets of information

 Essentials

Quick handy tips

 Questions

Answers to common questions

When you're done reading, you can finally
say you know **EVERYTHING®**!

PUBLISHER Karen Cooper

MANAGING EDITOR, EVERYTHING® SERIES Lisa Laing

COPY CHIEF Casey Ebert

ASSISTANT PRODUCTION EDITOR Alex Guarco

ACQUISITIONS EDITOR Pam Wissman

DEVELOPMENT EDITOR Brett Palana-Shanahan

EVERYTHING® SERIES COVER DESIGNER Erin Alexander

Visit the entire Everything® series at *www.everything.com*

THE

EVERYTHING®
Job Interview
Question
BOOK

The best answers to the
toughest interview questions

DAWN ROSENBERG McKAY

Avon, Massachusetts

To Rebecca: We've given you wings—now fly. We've given you roots—don't forget you'll always have a home. To Dean: Without your encouragement and support, having this career would not have been possible.

An Everything® Series Book.
Everything® and everything .com® are registered trademarks of F+W Media, Inc.

Published by Adams Media, a division of F+W Media, Inc.
57 Littlefield Street, Avon, MA 02322. U.S.A.
www.adamsmedia.com

Previous edition published as *The Everything® Practice Interview Book, 2nd Edition* by Dawn Rosenberg McKay, copyright © 2009, 2004 by F+W Media, Inc., ISBN 10: 1-60550-050-X, ISBN 13: 978-1-60550-050-8.

ISBN 10: 1-4405-6955-X
ISBN 13: 978-1-4405-6955-5
eISBN 10: 1-4405-6956-8
eISBN 13: 978-1-4405-6956-2

Printed in the United States of America.

10 9 8 7 6 5 4 3 2 1

Library of Congress Cataloging-in-Publication Data

McKay, Dawn Rosenberg.
The everything job interview question book / Dawn Rosenberg McKay.
pages cm. -- (Everything series)
Includes index.
ISBN-13: 978-1-4405-6955-5 (pbk.)
ISBN-10: 1-4405-6955-X (pbk.)
ISBN-10: 978-1-4405-6956-2 (ebook)
ISBN-10: 1-4405-6956-8 (ebook)
1. Employment interviewing. I. Title.
HF5549.5.I6M3268 2013
650.14'4--dc23

2013031072

Many of the designations used by manufacturers and sellers to distinguish their products are claimed as trademarks. Where those designations appear in this book and F+W Media was aware of a trademark claim, the designations have been printed with initial capital letters.

Cover image © istockphoto/bubaone.

This book is available at quantity discounts for bulk purchases. For information, please call 1-800-289-0963.

Contents

Top 10 Things Not to Say
on a Job Interview

1. That suit looks expensive! How much money do you make, anyway?
2. What will my salary be? My rent is very high!
3. I've never heard of this company before. What type of business is this?
4. It wasn't my fault I got fired. My boss always had it in for me.
5. I quit my job because my coworkers were all idiots. I didn't like working with any of them.
6. How much time do you give for maternity leave?
7. How much vacation time would I have? I need a lot of time off for traveling.
8. If someone files a sexual harassment charge against me, you'll have my back, right?
9. This isn't exactly what I want to be doing, but let's see what happens.
10. I'll really need to have my own office. I don't like working with other people.

Introduction

Wouldn't it be nice if you could send out your resume for a position you're qualified for and simply be offered a job? After all, everything about you is right there on your resume, isn't it? You should know—you put it there yourself.

But no, everything about you is not on your resume. Think of your resume as a pencil sketch of who you really are. There is no dimension to it. It has no color and no expression. Basically, it's pretty flat. Not at all like you; you are multifaceted. You've made choices throughout your career. You've reached certain goals and celebrated many accomplishments. You should have a chance to talk about all of that, because those details are what will make an employer want to hire you.

The job interview is your chance to show your prospective employer who you really are and what you can bring to the position. By asking you questions, a prospective employer can learn all about you and why you made the choices you made. He can discover what motivates you and what makes you proud. The interviewer can find out how you will fit in with his company. Will you get along with other employees? Will you make important contributions to his organization?

There is a lot to accomplish during the job interview. It's perhaps the most important part of the process; it's also the most difficult part. It's not like the resume you spent months poring over. You can edit your resume again and again until it lists the most important things about your career and uses the most effective wording to highlight your skills. However, a job interview usually takes place in less than an hour. When you say something, there's no delete key. If you forget to say something, the moment may have already passed by the time you realize it.

That is why it is so very important that you prepare well for the job interview. You won't have another chance to get it right, at least not with the same employer. The more comfortable you are with the entire process of interviewing, the more relaxed you will be when it comes time for the interview, and the better the interview will be.

This book will guide you through the entire job interview process, including everything you need to do before the interview takes place. Discover what you need to do to prepare for a job interview. Learn how to research a prospective employer so you can intelligently ask and answer questions during your interview. Find out how to dress for an interview. Learn about interviewing in another country.

The book is then packed full of sample job interview questions. For each question there is a great answer, an explanation of why you should give that answer, and then an answer you should never give and the reason why. As you go through the questions, think of how you would answer each one, using your own unique traits, experiences, and educational background.

Finally, you'll deal with the aftermath of the job interview. Find out what you need to do to follow up on a job interview. Is a thank-you letter really necessary? Of course, the whole purpose of this entire process is to get a job offer. Find out how to negotiate, accept, or reject one. By the time you're finished with this book, you'll be able to take on even the toughest interview.

CHAPTER 1

Preparing for the
Job Interview

Many people follow a certain routine when they are job hunting. They send copies of their resumes to prospective employers and follow that with weeks of sitting around, waiting to be called back. You should let your competition follow that routine—you can make much better use of your time! By preparing better in advance, you will increase your chances of getting hired when you finally do get that call.

Creating Opportunities

Preparing for interviews is time well spent, but only if you have interviews for which to get ready. Otherwise, it's like picking out your wedding attire without having a significant other! Let's first discuss what you are doing to create the opportunities to interview for jobs, beginning with locating job openings and presenting yourself as a candidate that gets the phone call (or e-mail) that includes the words "When can you come in to meet with us?"

These days, you should use online job boards and search engines like Monster.com, CareerBuilder.com, SimplyHired.com, and Indeed.com. In addition to searching for jobs on these sites, you can also post your resume so companies can find you. Many employers also use social media, such as Facebook, LinkedIn, and Twitter, to announce jobs.

Don't forget about networking, both face-to-face and social media. Personal connections are a good way to learn about job openings and spread the word that you are in the market for a new job.

Applying Online

The way we look for jobs has changed and so has how we apply for them. Few employers want you to mail a hard copy of your resume. They will usually ask you to submit online, either through their own site or the site where they advertised the job, like Monster.com or CareerBuilder.com. Alternatively, they might ask you to send it by e-mail.

This resume you're sending—what does it look like? If you haven't put one together in a while, you may only remember to include information about your past jobs, including the names of the companies, the dates you worked there, and a description of what you did. While all of that must be on your resume, how you present that information has changed. Many employers use automated applicant-management systems. Also called *applicant-tracking systems*, this computer software stores information about job candidates, including their resumes and cover letters. When you send your application material, it is very likely it will be stored in a program like this. Employers can then use the applicant-tracking system to search through all the resumes they have received to identify those candidates that have the qualifications they are seeking. Why should this matter to you? When you write your resume, you must make sure it includes keywords that will be caught by the system and flag you as a viable candidate. One way to make sure your resume includes the right words is to use one that you customize for each job opening. Read the announcement carefully, particularly the section that lists qualifications, and make sure to include those exact words in your resume. If you are uploading your resume to a job-search site in hopes that an employer will find you, read through announcements for jobs similar to the one you want and use keywords you find there.

You can make sure your resume gets noticed by including a summary in it. This will, in approximately three sentences placed near the top of your resume, tell a prospective employer why you are a good candidate for the job. Remember those qualifications discussed earlier? Make sure to include the ones that are the most desirable in your summary.

The resume that you submit online should be very simple. If it is complex, the applicant-management system software may have trouble reading it. Use an easy-to-read font like Courier or Times New Roman. Type size shouldn't be smaller than 10-point font or larger than 12-point font. Don't boldface, italicize, or underline text.

Now that you know where to look for job listings and how to use your resume to best present yourself, it's time to move along to the job interview. Hopefully, you'll have many. The better your understanding of this necessary, though often dreaded, part of the job search, the less nervous you will be. Minimizing your anxiety will allow you to be—and look, act, and sound—more confident. That's exactly how you want to appear on a job interview.

Understanding Job Interviews

Before you begin interviewing, make sure you have a good understanding of what interviews are all about. You should know about the interview process, the different types of interviews, and what employers are trying to learn about you from an interview. Becoming more knowledgeable about what to expect will help you demystify the entire interview process. This, in turn, will allow you to feel more confident when you are on a job interview. Remember, the more confident you are, the more confident you will look to your potential boss.

Getting to Know You

Have you ever wondered what the point of a job interview is? The employer has your resume—can't she just look at it to see whether you have the necessary skills and experience? All she has to do is make a phone call or two to verify that information, right? While your resume is made up of information about your past experience, it doesn't give the employer a full picture of who you are. Your resume is only a summary of your skills, work experience, and educational background. With only your resume to rely on, the employer won't have any idea of the specific things about you that will set you apart from the other candidates.

 Essential

> The interview is your chance to expand upon the facts you listed on your resume. Rather than thinking of an interview as an inquisition, you should instead look at it as a wonderful opportunity to express your true self to your prospective employer.

After all, a resume is merely a piece of paper, and you are so much more than that. An interviewer can't learn about someone's personality by looking at a resume. She can't discover how a candidate developed some of his skills or which accomplishments meant the most to him. The interviewer can't find out how the candidate reacts to change or adversity by reading his resume.

The only way an interviewer can learn any of those things about a job candidate is by talking to him and asking questions. This will allow the candidate to paint a picture of himself that is much more elaborate than what can fit on one sheet of paper.

Getting to Know Your Prospective Employer

Another purpose of a job interview is to help you to learn about the employer. You will discover things on a job interview that will allow you to make an informed decision about whether to accept or reject an offer should the employer make one. You will learn some things about the employer by asking questions. You will also learn things about the employer from the questions she asks you. For example, if the interviewer starts asking questions about working late or traveling, you can safely assume that these things will be part of your life if you get the job.

You may decide by the end of a job interview that this isn't really the job for you, or that this company isn't one you want to work for. And that's okay. It's in everyone's best interests, both the employer's and yours, to make this determination before you accept a job offer and begin working.

The Interview Process

The interview process can go on for quite a while. First, you may be asked to come in for a screening interview, which is your first interview with a particular employer. In some cases it may even take place over the telephone. During a screening interview, the person interviewing you will usually be someone in the human resources department, and he will want to verify items that are on your resume, such as dates of employment and schooling.

If the person who completes your screening interview is satisfied, he will most likely set up a selection interview. While someone from human resources may interview you again at this point, it is also likely that a department manager will interview you. The department manager, in addition to making sure you have the desirable skills and background, will want to make sure you have the right personality for the position.

Following the first selection interview, the employer may ask you to come back for subsequent interviews. During these further interviews, the employer may want to introduce you to other people in the company to make sure you are the right choice. Remember, you are still in the interviewing phase, so be on your best behavior.

 Question

What should I discuss on a second interview?
Use this opportunity to bring up something that you didn't get to talk about during the initial interview. Be prepared with an example of a specific skill or achievement you didn't have a chance to highlight before. Remember to explain how the example shows you are a good candidate for the particular position you want.

The employer may call back other candidates as she tries to narrow down her choices. Sometimes you will be the only candidate who is asked to return for more interviews. That usually is good news, but don't consider it a done deal until you actually have a job offer.

Preparing to Answer Questions

You will be asked a variety of questions on a job interview. These questions will pertain to your skills and abilities, accomplishments, education, and work history. You will also be asked questions about your strengths and weaknesses, your interests and hobbies, and your likes and dislikes, all of which will allow the employer to learn about your personal traits or characteristics.

Later in the book, you will find questions you might encounter on a job interview. While answers (both good and bad) are given, they are only guidelines. You should try to figure out how you will answer those questions. While you should not go into a job interview with a memorized script, you should have an idea of how you will answer most questions that will come your way. This book will give you ideas for the types of questions you should ask the interviewer. Use these questions in the same way—as a guideline you can adapt to your particular situation, the company with which you are interviewing, and the industry it is in.

Learning about Yourself

Your goal on a job interview is to give the best answers you can possibly give. In order to do that, there's someone you need to get to know—yourself. You probably worked hard at putting together a great resume that highlights your skills, accomplishments, and experience. This was time well spent, since a great resume will help you line up the right interview. There is, however, only so much you can get across in a resume. You need to uncover what is behind that basic outline so you can present it to the interviewer and show him what an excellent candidate you really are.

Be Specific

Be prepared to give detailed answers to job interview questions. The interviewer, for example, will ask you about your skills. You know what skills you have, but can you discuss how you acquired them? What if the interviewer asks you about your accomplishments? You've no doubt accomplished a lot at work, but can you recall specifics? You will need to use anecdotes that clearly back up any claims you've made on your resume or that you make during the interview, so it is imperative that you prepare some. Look back at some of your experiences and get ready to provide good examples of your strengths when the subject comes up.

Go Beyond the Resume

The interviewer will likely use your resume to guide him through the interview. Study your resume in order to become intimately familiar with each item you have listed on it. You must be prepared to talk about and elaborate on every item on it, since a resume by definition is just a brief summary of your work history. To keep it succinct, you only provided the most pertinent of details about your experience.

 Fact

Interviewers generally expect more than yes or no answers to their questions. You must give details that clearly explain your answer. When an interviewer asks you to discuss a particular situation, be ready to give a specific answer and expand upon it with brief examples.

On a job interview, by contrast, the interviewer expects you to elaborate. Sit down with a clean copy of your resume and a notebook in front of you. Look at each job you have listed on your resume and think about every single one carefully, one at a time. What do you remember about the job? Do you remember why you started working there and why you left? What was it like working there? Take notes so you can study them later.

You should try to recall details about the job beyond what you put on your resume. Did your boss rely on you to perform certain duties because of a particular strength you possess? Can you recall times when you were invaluable to your employer?

 Alert

> Don't exaggerate on your resume. If the information on your resume isn't completely true, it will be impossible for you to discuss it during a job interview without continuing to exaggerate or lie. By the time you are done, if you have not been caught, you will have presented yourself as a totally different person than who you really are.

Do you remember which job was your favorite (or least favorite)? Can you recall what you liked (or disliked) about each one? Think about some projects you worked on. What skills did you use in order to complete those projects? What obstacles did you have to overcome to complete them? Did you most often work on a team, or did you usually work alone? Can you give examples of projects you worked on as part of a team and those you worked on independently?

A solid resume will list your major accomplishments. Try to remember what effort you put into achieving each one. Did the accomplishment help you reach a goal? How did it benefit the employer? Were you in any way rewarded for your achievement, perhaps with a promotion? If you take the time to recall this information before your interview, you won't have to worry about long silences as you try to remember facts while the pressure is on.

Clean Up Your Online Profile

Unfortunately, a prospective employer may be able to learn more about you than you would like by simply plugging your name into a search engine like Yahoo! or Google. Of course, the best way to prevent anyone from finding something embarrassing about you is by not putting anything online that could be. That includes pictures of you drinking or doing drugs, or anything that implies that you do or did drink excessively or take drugs. That means no pictures of you holding or standing next to drug paraphernalia or bottles of alcoholic beverages, passed out or hugging the porcelain god or looking visibly inebriated or stoned. Is it too late? Are there already pictures like this floating around out there? If they are on your own social media page, remove them immediately. If you are tagged in photographs like these on someone else's page, un-tag yourself. Don't forget to check all the social media sites you currently use as well as the ones you once did. Don't forget about video- and photo-sharing sites. Plug your own name into a search engine to see what others could find. Sure, you might find that you share the same name with a hundred people, and some have left quite the dirty footprint online, but at least you'll be aware of it and can explain that it's not you. If you find something you think might portray you poorly, send an e-mail and ask (maybe even beg) whoever has control over the content to take it down. Don't forget to be polite, and if it can help you make your case, contrite.

Take Time to Rehearse

To prepare for job interviews, it is important that you do some practice interviews, both alone and with others. Rehearsing for interviews will allow you to work on any problems that could affect the interviewers' opinion of you. Rehearsing will also allow you to become more comfortable with the interview process. By the time you go on an interview, you will have no problem confidently answering questions.

The interview is not only about what you say, but also about how you say it. It is difficult to see yourself as you appear to others. When you are engaged in conversation with someone, do you tend to look disinterested or do you generally look engaged? Do you look nervous or calm? Do you talk too fast, too slowly, too softly, or too loudly? You probably don't know the answers to these questions unless someone has pointed out a problem to you in the past.

To get a glimpse of what you look like when you are having a conversation with someone, you might want to begin rehearsing for your job interview in front of a mirror. Study your body language.

Are your hands clasped tightly in your lap? Are your arms folded across your chest? Are you smiling? Remember, your body language speaks volumes.

Next, recruit a friend to help. If you know someone who has experience interviewing others, especially someone who is responsible for hiring, ask him to work with you. If that person is unavailable, find someone else whose opinion you trust. Have him ask you questions and then answer them as if you were on an actual interview. To make the situation more realistic, have your friend choose the questions to ask.

If you have friends who are job hunting, you can all practice interviewing together. Record videos of yourselves interviewing each other, and play them back. Critique other performances as well as your own. Once you get through that, the real thing will seem so much easier.

Dealing with Anxiety

Interviews make lots of people nervous. With anxiety levels from mild to severe, it can sabotage your performance on a job interview. Many people fear the unknown most, so preparing for a job interview can help alleviate this feeling. With that said, you may still have butterflies fluttering around in your stomach, despite becoming as familiar as possible with the interview process, learning what questions to anticipate, thinking about how you will answer them, and rehearsing for the interview. If you've done everything you can to prepare, you have significantly increased your chances of succeeding, so remember that. You should be able to walk into the interview calm, cool, collected, and bursting with confidence. However, you won't be able to do that if you aren't relaxed. Don't let your anxiety take away from your performance on a job interview. Find a way to relieve your stress, before it affects your chances of getting the job you want.

People use many techniques to relieve stress. You should know which techniques work well for you, and use them in the days leading up to your interview. Many people swear by exercise as a great way to relieve anxiety. If exercise is one of the ways you de-stress, an early morning run before an interview, or a workout at the gym, may help. If strenuous exercise isn't something you are used to, it may not be wise to start a new exercise regimen the day of your interview. Instead, perhaps a tension-relieving walk around town, would be better. You can also try massage, meditation, or deep breathing.

 Fact

A change in employment is consistently ranked as one of the most stressful life events. With that in mind, it's perfectly normal to be anxious about a job interview.

What to Do about Low Confidence

Sometimes job searches can take a very long time. This is especially true during economic downturns. People are sometimes out of work for months, or even years, which can be rough on a person's ego. If you are in this situation, your confidence may wane, and you may doubt whether you will ever find a job.

Your lack of confidence will be visible to anyone you come into contact with—including employers. You must get out of your slump fast, or you won't be hired—not because of a bad economy, but because of the way you carry yourself.

Zoom in on your accomplishments. Remember all the great things you did in your career. Think about what you can bring to a new job. Think about how lucky any employer would be to have you work for her. Focus on these things, and the interviewer will notice them too.

CHAPTER 2

Learning about Your Prospective Employer

Ralph Waldo Emerson said, "There is no knowledge that is not power." Make this your mantra as you prepare for job interviews, especially if you're wondering whether it's worthwhile to research prospective employers. Be assured—the time and effort spent gathering information is a wise investment. In business, corporations do research to find out information about clients and competitors because it helps them compete, which can result in higher sales and increased profits. Your commitment to researching prospective employers can result in performing better in interviews than competitors. An added benefit is that, when it comes time to entertain an offer from an employer, you'll have data to help make an informed decision.

What Do You Need to Know?

Before you begin to think that researching prospective employers will be an enormous task, remember that, unless you're planning to write an extensive treatise on a company, you don't need to know everything there is to know about it. You only need to know some basic information.

First, you want a company description. Find out what the company does (i.e., what products or services it sells), to whom it sells, and in what industry the company operates. You may be interviewing for a sales job, but you should know whether you would be selling cosmetics to drugstores or tools to mechanics.

 Alert

Companies often hire professional librarians to do their research. You won't have that luxury, so you are encouraged to learn how to perform this task on your own. You can, of course, visit your local public library or college library and receive assistance there. Librarians will acquaint you with the research tools they have available.

Look at the organizational structure of the company. Is it a subsidiary of another one, or is it a parent company? If it is the latter, find out what companies are its subsidiaries. Learn about a company's key personnel. You don't have to find extensive biographies, but you should know names and a bit about top executives and those for whom you will be working, if you know who they are.

Having knowledge about a company's financial situation is important, both for the interview and for deciding whether to accept an offer of employment. After all, wouldn't you rather go to work for a company that is in good financial health than one that is struggling? Determine whether the company is privately or publicly held. The course of your research will very much depend on the answer to that question.

You should also know some details about a company's history. Find out what year the company was founded and by whom. Learn what the company's mission was and is. Has the company changed its focus over the years? Find out if the company ever faced any difficulties and how it overcame them.

Knowing about a company's past is important, but you also want to know about its present. It is imperative to stay on top of the latest news about your prospective employer, the industry, and your profession. Find out if there are any changes on the horizon, such as mergers or acquisitions, and what effect these changes will have on the company and its employees. You should learn whether the company has released any new products lately and how the public has reacted to these products. You should be aware of any changes that are occurring in the industry and in your profession as well.

 Essential

If you have been away from your career for an extended period of time, it is especially important that you keep up with any developments and changes in your field. A leave of absence from the workforce isn't an excuse to ignore current events.

Finally, don't walk into your interview without details about the job for which you are a candidate. If you don't have a job announcement, check the employer's website to see if you can find one there. It is perfectly appropriate for you to ask for a detailed job description when the employer calls to invite you to come in for an interview. The more you know about the job, the better you will be able to demonstrate to the employer that you are the best person to fill it.

Where to Begin Your Research

The easiest place to begin your research is the company's website. Most entities have websites, so it should be fairly easy to find the one you're looking for. Use a search engine like Google or Yahoo! and type the organization's name in quotation marks into the search box. In addition to finding the company's official site, your results may also bring up other sites that talk about your prospective employer. Bookmark those sites to look at when you get further into your research. Remember that the primary purpose of a corporate website is to act as a publicity tool. The information you find there is meant to cast the company in the best possible light, so don't expect to dig up any dirt there.

Next, if the organization you are researching is publicly held, meaning it has publicly traded securities, you should try to get your hands on its annual report and other corporate documents.

According to U.S. law, most publicly held companies are required to disclose financial and other pertinent information to their shareholders and to the Securities and Exchange Commission.

 Fact

> Do you want to figure out which website on your results list belongs to the company? Look at the URLs listed there—the company's URL will often include the company's name. For example, the URL for Adams Media, the publisher of this book, is *www.adamsmedia.com*.

These companies send glossy, magazine-style annual reports to shareholders. While these reports must be accurate, companies sometimes spin the facts in their annual reports. For a more detailed and more realistic look, see the reports your prospective employer files with the SEC. These corporate reports are filed after the end of a company's fiscal year, quarterly, and whenever an event warrants disclosure.

 Alert

> Most publicly held companies must file annual, quarterly, or other reports with the SEC, but some don't have to after the end of the fiscal year they first went public. Only companies with more than $10 million in assets and securities held by more than 500 shareholders, or companies with fewer than 300 shareholders, must file with the SEC. If the company for which you need information is relatively small, you must use other sources.

You can often find the annual report on a company's website or you can request a copy from its investor relations department. You can download most other corporate reports from the SEC's website (*www.sec.gov*) through the EDGAR database. Look for an annual report called a 10-K and a quarterly report called a 10-Q. Current information, such as earnings announcements, are reported in 8-Ks.

If a company isn't required to report earnings and other information to the SEC, it may be difficult to find its financial reports. Privately held companies do not have to disclose this information; therefore they often do not. With a little digging you might be able to find limited financial information about your prospective employer, such as annual sales.

Company Directories

One place to look for information about an organization's finances is in a company directory. These are encyclopedia- or dictionary-style resources that contain entries on many different companies. While they don't contain a wealth of information, they do cover the basics. For example, you should be able to learn about a company's products and services, its monetary value, its key personnel, and its organizational structure.

Company directories are generally available online at most public and college libraries. Patrons and students can access them from their home computers as well as on site. For more about that, consult with your library. A librarian can tell you which directories they subscribe to and can teach you how to use them.

Keeping Up with the News

Some of the information you find may be outdated. This is especially true of print resources—some online databases are frequently updated. Even annual and quarterly reports only give you information as of a particular date. And by the time they are released, the data contained in them is typically a few months old. In your research, you may have learned that your prospective employer manufactures a particular product or provides a particular service. Recently, perhaps, that company has added a new product or service. Maybe that's even the reason they're hiring now. Your prospective employer may have just acquired a new subsidiary or may have been purchased by another company. Don't underestimate the importance of uncovering the latest news you can find, whether that news is positive or negative.

 Alert

> If you learn something that puts your prospective employer in a bad light, think carefully before bringing it up. If you need the information to decide whether to accept a job offer, ask your question as tactfully as you can: "I hope this doesn't offend you, but I really need to know the answer to this question."

News Search Engines

You can search for news stories using search engines like Google, Yahoo!, and Ask.com. Each has a news search function that is separate from its regular web search function. You will find stories listed there minutes after they break. You don't have to continually search these engines for breaking news; you can receive alerts whenever the search engine picks up something new.

You can receive news alerts by e-mail or through a newsfeed. The steps you need to take to do this vary by search engine. On Google, for example, go to Google Alerts (*www.google.com/alerts*), type in your search query, and indicate how often you would like to receive alerts and the address to which you want them delivered. On Yahoo! go to Yahoo! Alerts (alerts.yahoo.com) and click on the link that says "Keyword News." Type in your search term and then set up your desired frequency and means of delivery. Watch your mailbox for breaking news about the company or industry you are following.

Setting up a newsfeed takes some more effort, since you will have to sign up for a newsfeed reader or aggregator. A newsfeed reader goes to the sites to which you've subscribed and collects newly added content on your topic for you to read. This is an invaluable tool if you plan to subscribe to news from several different sources. It is also a must-have if you subscribe to any blogs, which will be discussed later. There are web-based newsfeed readers that you can access via a website, as well as ones that you can install on your computer or mobile device.

 ## Question

What newsfeed reader should I use?
Bloglines (*www.bloglines.com*) is a popular newsfeed reader. Once you set up an account, you can use the web browser on your computer or mobile device to subscribe to newsfeeds and blogs. Feedly (*www.feedly.com*), another newsfeed reader, is available as a browser extension for Firefox and Chrome and as a mobile app for the iOS (previously iPhone iOS) operating system and Android.

Once you have signed up for a newsfeed reader, you can subscribe to a newsfeed. First perform your search and then, on your results page, look for a link to subscribe to the feed. It may say "RSS" (which stands for Really Simple Syndication), "Atom," or "Subscribe to this search." Clicking on the link will bring you to the subscription page of your newsfeed reader.

Blogs

You will also use a newsfeed reader to subscribe to and read blogs. A blog is an abbreviation for web log, and it is traditionally an online journal or diary. Although in the past blogs were maintained primarily by people who wanted to share details of their personal lives or opinions on any number of topics, they have moved into the mainstream over the last few years. Now, corporations maintain official blogs and often link to them on their websites. You can find company news there, or at least news that the company wants to share with the general public. In addition to reading official company blogs, you should be very interested in perusing blogs maintained by employees—or former employees.

You can easily find blogs about any topic using blog search engines. Google and Ask.com both have blog search engines among their tools. Technorati (*www.technorati.com*) is a search engine dedicated specifically to blogs. In addition to finding complete blogs on your topic, you can also find individual posts on blogs that cover more general topics. If you locate a blog you find interesting, you can subscribe to it.

 Alert

> A blog kept by an employee or former employee may be filled with gossip, but you may be able to find some grains of truth. Read these blogs with a critical eye, remembering there may be inaccuracies in them. Disgruntled former employees, for example, may not say the nicest of things. Some statements may be true and others may not.

Social Networking Sites

Social networking sites have done a lot to change how to connect with the people in your life. Did you know you could also use them to learn about prospective employers? You can "follow" companies' and organizations' official Twitter (*www.twitter.com*) or LinkedIn (*www.linkedin.com*) pages or "like" pages on Facebook. The same way you see your college roommate's status about his "really fun weekend" show up in your feed, so will a prospective employer's update about a new product it just introduced.

Access Your Network

A network is a group of individuals to whom you can turn for help. Your network may consist of people you've worked with in the past, your friends, and your relatives. These people have networks of their own and may know others who can give you advice. Eventually, if you branch out far enough, you're bound to find someone who knows something about one of the companies you're interested in.

Online networking can be helpful. Where else can you connect with former classmates, parents of your children's current classmates, your sister-in-law's brother's best friend, and your coworker from your very first job—all in one place? You never know which of these relationships will come in handy when you are trying to find out about job openings or learn about employers before big interviews. However, while Facebook is great for keeping up with friends and family, LinkedIn is the way to go for professional networking. LinkedIn users post content that is relevant to their careers, not their dining experiences, their vacations, or their kids.

 Alert

> Be cautious about revealing anything you learned through your network. If you start talking about something not released to the public, the interviewer will want to know how you got your information. Your network can be valuable for gaining information, and for getting an inside peek at a work environment, but be careful about how you use it.

Once you sign up for an account, you can build a profile that includes information about your professional life—similar to what is on your resume. Then, start connecting with people you know. You can search for them by typing their names, one by one, into the search box, and then send them a request to connect. However, it's easier to have LinkedIn search your e-mail contact list to find people who are using the site. Simply click on the Add Connections icon (in the upper right corner, the little profile with a plus sign to the left of it), follow the prompts to connect with your e-mail list, and select those with whom you want to connect.

While there is a generic message that pops up when you indicate you want to connect with someone on LinkedIn, you should send one that is personalized. Keep it simple, but explain why you are inviting him or her to connect. What should you do if you want to connect with someone but don't know him or her personally? See if that person is connected to someone you know, and request an introduction. Most people think of their networks only when they are trying to find out about employment opportunities. However, a great time to access your network is when you have been asked to come in for a job interview. Some members of your contacts may have worked for the company you are interviewing with, and others may know someone who has worked there, or who currently works there. Someone in your network may have interviewed there in the past, or may know the person who is interviewing you.

Imagine all the valuable information you can get from someone who has had some sort of contact with the company you are interviewing with. You can learn things you would not be able to learn anywhere else. Sure, you can use other resources to gather information about a company's finances or to find up-to-date news. Someone on your network, though, may be able to tell you that the person who is interviewing you will be very impressed by the fact that you speak four languages and will tell you not to wear anything green, because the interviewer really hates it.

CHAPTER 3

First Impressions Count

You have worked hard researching your prospective employer, and you know what you need to say to convince him you are the best candidate for the job. But there's one more thing to think about before the big day: the first impression. Your physical appearance, what you do when you meet the interviewer, and your body language during the interview all contribute to the opinion your interviewer will form about you. Be prepared to make a great first impression even before you open your mouth.

What to Wear to the Interview

Most people are troubled by the thought of what to wear for a job interview. They wonder if they should wear casual clothes or formal attire. They question whether to choose bright colors or neutral tones. Even among professional stylists, there is quite a bit of disagreement over what is appropriate to wear for a job interview.

Some experts feel that regardless of the culture of the company, a person should always wear a suit. Other experts feel that wearing a suit is not necessary in some situations; worse, it could even be inappropriate. Are you even more confused now? Don't be. Here are some pointers for choosing an outfit that will help you shine on a job interview.

When Should You Wear a Suit?

If you are interviewing for a job in a traditionally conservative field, such as accounting, finance, or law, the answer to the question "What should I wear?" is a simple one. Both men and women must wear suits. You should choose a conservative color like black, dark gray, or navy.

Invest in at least two suits. If you buy two, you won't have to worry about what to wear when you get called back for a second interview. You will also be a step ahead when you get a job offer and those suits become a regular part of your wardrobe. Buy a conservative rather than a trendy suit, and always buy the best quality you can afford. You can wear the same suit for several years if you stick to these rules.

 Fact

If you want to get the best prices on business attire, remember that men's suits are often on sale during April and November. Men's shirts go on sale in January and July, and the best months to buy shoes are January, July, November, and December.

Underneath the suit, you should wear a preferably white or light-colored solid shirt or blouse. A man should wear a necktie; a woman can accessorize with a silk scarf if she wishes. Both ties and scarves should have simple designs and should not be too brightly colored. Women's scarves should be of short or medium length, since a long scarf could get in her way.

Is Casual Dress Ever Appropriate?

Your choices of what to wear are limited when you are interviewing in a conservative field. That is not necessarily a bad thing—at least it makes your decision easier. Just ask anyone who is interviewing for a job in a field where the mode of dress is not so clearly defined. The definition of proper interview attire in a casual office is something not all experts agree on, whether you ask those who work in fashion or those who work in career planning.

While some people feel that a formal suit is appropriate for all job interviews, others feel that what you wear on an interview should be similar to what you will wear on the job. When you have a job interview, you want the interviewer to envision you as a member of his staff. The way you dress can help him do that.

 Essential

If you can't find a company's dress code standards through traditional research, hanging out near the building's entrance at the beginning of a work day will allow you to see what people look like when they arrive for work. Avoid doing this on a Friday, as that is the day of the week many companies allow casual dress.

Of course, a job interview should be considered a special occasion and not just a typical day at the office. Therefore, your attire should be a notch or two above what you would wear to work. If, for example, typical dress in the workplace you're interested in joining is casual, men should opt for dress pants and a coordinating sport jacket, and women should wear dress pants, a skirt, or a dress and coordinated blazer.

A company's corporate culture usually dictates how employees dress. You can try to learn more about a prospective employer's corporate culture from the research you do in preparation for the job interview. Companies in more creative industries usually have less stringent dress codes.

If you have exhausted all ways of finding out how employees of the company dress, you might have to wear a suit. If given the choice between overdressing for a job interview and underdressing for one, you are better off being overdressed. In other words, it is more acceptable to be the only job candidate who shows up in a suit rather than the only one who does not.

The Finer Details

More important than what you wear to a job interview is how you wear it. Check your clothing to make sure it is stain-free. Also make sure it is unwrinkled. The last thing you want is to look like you rolled out of the hamper. It is worth bringing your suit to the dry cleaner to have it professionally cleaned and pressed.

 Alert

Women should make sure their hosiery is free of runs and visible snags. Carry an extra pair in your purse just in case. Men should make sure their tie is straight. Invest in a tie tack to keep it in place.

Women should stay away from low-cut necklines or skirts with short hemlines. Revealing outfits may be fine for an evening out after work, but they are not appropriate for the office—any office. Suits should fit properly. That means they should not be too tight or too baggy. If your outfit does not fit you well, a trip to the tailor is in order.

Hair, Makeup, and Nails

Make sure your hair is neat, clean, and simply styled. Women—don't overdo your makeup, and use lipstick and nail polish that isn't too brightly colored. Women's nails should be short enough to keep the interviewer from wondering, "How will she get work done with those nails?" Men's nails should be short and clean. Men should either be clean-shaven or have neatly trimmed facial hair.

Guidelines for Jewelry

Both men and women should keep jewelry to a minimum. That means large dangling earrings, big pendants, and thick chains are out. While body piercings and tattoos may be all the rage in your social circle, remember that this will turn off some interviewers. Make sure they are under your clothing if possible. While you are allowed to have your own personal style, a job interview may not be the best place for you to express it. You certainly do not want anything to distract the interviewer from realizing you are the best candidate for the job.

Your Shoes

Finally, it's time to think about your feet, or rather what you are going to put on them. Your shoes are the last things you will put on before you head off on an interview, but they should not be the last things you think about. On the contrary, give serious consideration to your footwear.

Shoes that are conservative in both style and color are the most appropriate to wear on a job interview. Neither men nor women should wear sandals or open-toed shoes of any kind. Black shoes go with everything, even with navy, according to fashion experts.

 Fact

One of the first things some job interviewers notice is the condition of a candidate's shoes. Scuffed, dirty shoes may indicate that the person doesn't pay attention to detail. You can purchase shoe polish and other shoe-care supplies at your local drug store.

Shoes must be in good condition. They do not have to be brand-new, but they should not look like you have hiked miles in them, either. They shouldn't have scuffs on them; if they do, polish them. If you buy new shoes for the interview, make sure they are comfortable. It is hard to concentrate on the task at hand when your toes are being pinched. Excessively high heels are out of place on a job interview and in the workplace.

What to Bring to the Interview

Once you are dressed appropriately, you are ready to walk into the interview with confidence. There are a few things you should always have with you. First and foremost, always bring along a few copies of your resume. The interviewer may want a fresh copy, and you may be introduced to other people who will need one as well. In order to keep your resumes clean and neat, put them in a folder to transport them to the interview.

You may have a portfolio of work samples; if the interviewer has asked to see them or if you think they are noteworthy, bring them with you. Make sure they are neatly compiled and organized. They should represent your best work.

 Essential

Arrange your work samples in a binder. The binder should be a conservative color, such as black or navy, and it should be in good condition. Insert your documents into plastic sheet protectors, which you can find at all office supply stores.

Always carry a pen and a small notebook in case there is something you want to jot down. Do not forget to bring your date book, if it isn't in your phone, so you can schedule any future appointments.

Carry your resumes, portfolio, and other items in a briefcase. Women may also carry small purses. In general, travel light. Don't carry bulky handbags or backpacks, and shopping bags are definitely out.

Getting to the Interview on Time

There is one thing you can do to sabotage your chances of getting hired even before you shake the interviewer's hand. If you arrive late for the interview, you might as well write your own rejection letter. Your prospective employer will be offended. Even showing up exactly on time is a bad idea. Running in at the last minute will throw you off, and you will not perform as well as you might have, had you arrived with a few minutes to spare. There are a few things you can do to reduce your risk of being late.

When a prospective employer calls to ask you to come in for an interview, be sure to find out exactly where the interview will take place. Some companies have offices in more than one location. These addresses can be across town or merely across the street from one another. Regardless of the distance between them, you do not want to waste time wandering from one place to another.

 Fact

Plan your trip online using mapping websites or a smartphone app. Municipal transit systems post their schedules and routes online and many even have apps. You can type in your starting point and your destination, using landmarks, addresses, or intersections, to plan your trip.

Once you know where you have to go, you have to figure out how to get there. If you are driving, map out a route and, if possible, an alternate route just in case you hit some traffic snags along the way. If you have to take a train or a bus, make sure you know which lines you have to ride and which ones you can ride instead if something should happen to interrupt service.

You should plan to arrive for your interview early. It is best to get there at least ten or fifteen minutes before your scheduled appointment. If you decide to be an early bird, though, do not show up inside your prospective employer's office any more than ten to fifteen minutes prior to your appointment. Doing so may make the interviewer feel like you are pressuring her to start the interview early.

Arriving for Your Appointment

Announce yourself to the receptionist as soon as you arrive at your prospective employer's office. Many people do not realize how important this part is. The receptionist is the first employee of the company with whom you and all the other interviewees will have contact. Do not underestimate the power this person wields. The interviewer may rely on the receptionist to give an opinion of the job candidates. That is one reason it is imperative that you be on your very best behavior right from the start. You might also wind up working with this person.

Politely walk up to the reception desk, give the receptionist your name, and the name of the person with whom you have an appointment. You can make small talk about the weather or traffic if you wish. Remember, if you are kept waiting, do not complain to the receptionist or become argumentative with him.

While you are waiting to be called in for the interview, spend your time wisely. You can look over your resume and review any notes you may have prepared. If you finish doing that and still have not been called in, take a look at the professional journals that may be available in the waiting area. Do not bring out the novel you brought along to read on the train. You want to look like you are busy, not as if you are relaxing.

The Interview Begins

Usually the receptionist will announce your arrival to the interviewer, and she will come out to the waiting area to greet you. This is the only chance you will have to make a good first impression. While your behavior during the interview is important, a bad first impression will be very difficult to overcome.

Meeting the Interviewer

When you first meet the interviewer, you must appear confident, but not smug. Be assertive, but not aggressive; friendly, but not overly familiar.

When the interviewer comes out to greet you, the first thing you must do is introduce yourself to him using your first and last name. Do not address him by his first name. Your introduction should sound something like this (feel free to use your own variation): "Hello, Mr. Smith. I'm Joan Brown. It's nice to meet you." You should be ready to shake his hand, but do not offer your hand first. Doing so can put you in an awkward situation if the interviewer does not offer his hand in return.

Once you arrive in the office where your interview will be held, etiquette dictates that you wait for the interviewer to offer you a seat. However, just because someone is in a position to interview you does not mean he has manners. If the interviewer sits down without first offering you a seat, sit down across from him or take whatever seat is available. He is probably in a hurry to get the interview started so do not waste any time. Get the copies of your resume, portfolio, notebook, and pen ready so you won't have to fumble around trying to find them later.

 Fact

As you proceed to the site of the interview, the interviewer may try to make small talk. Stick to things like the weather and stay away from how your favorite team played last night. Your favorite team may turn out to be his team's archrival, which could result in an awkward moment you don't really need at this point.

Body Language

When you interact with other people, there are two ways your message comes through to them. You consciously convey your message through your words, and your body language unconsciously sends signals as well. Body language is comprised of the nonverbal gestures and mannerisms that may indicate a person's true feelings.

Your body language can reveal things that your words do not. In fact, it may reveal much more than you intend to. In the simplest terms, if you say you are happy but have a big frown on your face, your body language—the frown—will show your true feelings. While most people manage to exert a great deal of control over the words they let cross their lips, many have difficulty when it comes to keeping their body language in check.

You may think all this talk about body language is just a bunch of nonsense. In spite of that, pay attention to what your body language seems to reveal even if you question whether there is any truth to it. Many interviewers are trained to look for even the subtlest nonverbal cues and interpret what they mean. Whether these interpretations are correct is irrelevant; what the interviewer believes is what counts. Read the following section carefully. If you have a habit of doing anything that may make you appear anxious or disinterested, you need to extinguish that behavior.

 Essential

Do a mock job interview and record it on video. Analyze your body language afterward. Once you are able to see how you interact with others, you can work on identifying and eliminating any undesirable behavior that may be distracting in a job interview.

Stay Calm—or at Least Look That Way

A job interview is very stressful for many people. Your anxiety may be brought on by the fact that it is a very unnatural situation. How often do you sit across from another person while she fires a series of questions at you?

It is disconcerting to be put under a microscope, especially when your livelihood may depend on the outcome of that person's research. Since one of your goals on a job interview is to appear confident, the last thing you want to do is let your body language betray your anxiety.

What to Do with Your Hands and Arms

Many people do not know what to do with their hands and arms during an interview. Should you clasp them together or keep them at your sides? Should you hold a pen to keep your hands occupied? Should you keep your arms folded across your chest?

The best thing to do with your hands is to let them rest in your lap. You may keep them clasped together as long as you don't grip them too tightly and appear to be trying to hold them still. Folding your arms across your chest is often seen as an indication that you are closing yourself off or putting up a barrier. Since you want to appear open and approachable on a job interview, avoid doing that.

Holding a pen is not necessarily bad, but be careful not to fiddle with it. Remember not to point or clench your hands into fists. Also avoid covering your mouth with your hand or touching your face when you speak.

Make Eye Contact

If you have ever taken a public-speaking class, it was no doubt discussed how important it is to make eye contact. If you avoid making eye contact, the interviewer may jump to the conclusion that you are not being truthful about something. That, of course, is the last thing you would want an interviewer to determine from your body language. He may also be wary of hiring someone who appears to have difficulty carrying on a conversation, which is another impression you must avoid making.

 Essential

If you tend to be shy, or if making eye contact tends to be a problem for you, you can practice looking into the eyes of people you are very comfortable with when you talk to them. Graduate to making eye contact with the cashier in the supermarket or the bank teller. Soon you should be able to accomplish this in all situations.

Sit Up Straight

How you sit during an interview is very important. Think back to when you were a child and your parents and teachers told you to sit up straight. They were not kidding. Good posture helps you look confident. Slouching makes you look lazy and bored.

Sitting up straight also makes it easier to breathe, as any yoga instructor will tell you. Many people tend to forget to breathe when they are in a stressful situation, and they let out a huge sigh when they remember. This is not a good idea during an interview.

It is preferable to keep your feet flat on the floor, but you can also have them crossed at the ankles. Do not cross your legs at the knee or have your ankle resting on your opposite knee. You should lean forward slightly. This shows that you are an eager participant in the conversation.

The Handshake

Another important thing to think about is the handshake. The opportunity for a handshake presents itself at two points in a job interview. The first time is when you meet the interviewer. The other is at the end of the interview, when you are getting ready to leave.

Determining when a handshake should happen can be tricky. For instance, you might put out your hand and the gesture is not reciprocated, or the interviewer may extend her hand and you aren't ready to shake it. It can create an awkward situation and is certainly something you want to avoid.

Therefore, while you do not want to initiate the handshake, make sure you are ready for it by keeping your right hand free at your side, ready to move into the handshake position. Don't hold anything in that hand as you enter and leave the office. When you do shake, your handshake should be firm, which demonstrates that you are confident.

Making Your Exit

Just as your arrival at the interview provides you with your first opportunity to make a good impression, your exit provides you with the chance to make a lasting one. What you do at this point may be what sticks in the interviewer's mind when it is time to decide whom to hire. Make sure you end the interview on a positive note.

Do You Have Any Questions?

At the end of the interview, the interviewer will usually ask you if you have any questions. "No" is the wrong answer. This is your chance to become a proactive part of the job interview, so don't waste it. The purpose of your questions is twofold. They should indicate your interest in the job. They should also help you learn as much as you can to help you make an informed decision if you are offered the job. Prepare a short list of questions in advance so you won't be stuck wondering what to ask.

You can ask the interviewer to clarify the job duties, explain the chain of command, or for more information about something she mentioned during the interview. You will find a list of suggested questions later in this book.

 Alert

> When asking your prospective employer questions at the end of your interview, you should not ask questions about salary, vacations, or benefits. All of these topics are best left for when the employer offers you the job. It is more polite, and you will be in a better position to negotiate once you have received an offer.

Ask for the Job

Don't forget to ask for the job before you leave. Most people neglect to do this. They may not want to appear overly eager. However, the interviewer is not a mind reader. If you do not let him know you want the job, he may assume you have decided you don't want it.

You do not have to come out and say, "I want the job." You can say instead, "Based on what we discussed today, I think I would be a perfect fit for this job. When can I expect to hear from you?" This statement not only expresses your interest in the job, but also gives you the opportunity to reiterate that you are qualified to fill the position. Before you leave, say goodbye to the interviewer. Tell her it was nice to meet with her, and again be ready to shake the interviewer's hand if she extends it.

CHAPTER 4

Special Kinds of Interviews

Interviewing remotely, by phone or video conference, has become more and more common over the past few years, so you definitely need to be prepared for that possibility. You might even be asked to interview over a meal, which presents its own issues, as does interviewing in a foreign country, where the customs are likely to be different from what you are used to. All of these situations have different considerations that need to be taken into account.

Interviewing Remotely

Instead of asking job candidates to come into an office or meet in person somewhere else, more and more employers are instead choosing to conduct interviews by telephone or by video chat, using a program like Skype. Remote interviews are particularly common for screening interviews. This is your first interview with an employer, and usually someone from the human resources department, or sometimes a hiring manager, will verify the information on your resume. Follow-up interviews may even take place remotely, but it is likely you will eventually have to make your way into the office. Often prospective employers want to wait until they narrow down their list of candidates before bringing them into the office. They have a variety of reasons for using remote interviewing methods. The most common one is to save on the travel expenses associated with interviewing candidates who live out of town. Some even recognize that it is difficult for people who are currently employed to take time away from their jobs to travel, especially if their bosses don't know they are looking for new work. Others may want to keep their staffs out of the loop. They don't want their own employees to know they are conducting a candidate search.

Interviewing remotely is, in many ways, easier for a job candidate. You don't have to figure out how to get to the interview site or disrupt your schedule for more than a couple of hours. In the case of a telephone interview, you don't have to worry too much about your appearance, although for a video interview it is just as important as it is for an in-person one. However, don't be fooled into thinking a remote interview is in any way easier. There are things you have to think about when you are going to be interviewed by telephone or video chat that wouldn't be a concern if you were going to be interviewed in person.

Telephone Interviews

When you find out you're going to have a telephone interview, your first thought may be "Great! I don't even have to change out of my pajamas." Before you decide to run with that decision, please answer this question: How professional do you feel in your pajamas? You may feel more relaxed, and that's not a bad thing, but do you feel like you're ready to present your best self? Do you feel bright-eyed and enthusiastic? Do you have a lot of energy, or do you feel like you're ready to go back to bed? While you don't have to wear a suit for a phone interview—unless, of course, you want to—you should at least put on something you would wear outside. This will put you in the right frame of mind. Don't underestimate how important that is and how much it can figure into your success on an interview.

Some people find the telephone more intimidating than an in-person meeting. For one thing, you can't see the interviewer's facial expressions as he or she reacts to your answers. Is she interested in what you're saying? Does he seem to be impressed or dismayed?

Does it look like she wants you to keep going or stop talking? Those are all things you might be able to discern if you were sitting across from someone but nearly impossible to recognize over the phone. You can try to make an assumption based on the interviewer's tone, but that doesn't always work. Not everyone gives away his or her feelings this way, and trying to read something into someone's voice that may or may not be there will just make you anxious. Accept the fact that you won't be able to tell how the interviewer is reacting to your answers and do your best in spite of that. There are other things to concentrate on, in addition to how you answer questions that will contribute to your emerging victorious from a phone interview.

The most important thing to attend to is your environment. You must find a quiet place to talk. It will be very distracting, to both you and the interviewer, if you are interrupted. One interruption is one too many! Warn the people with whom you share a living space that, short a life-threatening emergency, they are not to disturb you. They must not try to interact with you by talking, pantomiming, or doing anything else to get your attention while you're on the phone. They should not even be in the same room; if you have a lock on the door, use it. If you have children, send them to a friend or babysitter unless they are old enough to understand how important it is for them to stay out of the way and be very quiet. Lock your pets in another room. Turn off music and the television. Do not look at any screen during your interview. That includes your phone screen and your computer screen. If you can't help yourself and need to peek, just turn everything off. Disable call waiting, and if you have any other phones in the room, switch their ringers off.

Don't eat or chew anything during a phone interview. You can sip water, however, to keep your mouth from getting dry. Sit up straight. This keeps your breathing regular and helps to keep you from losing focus as you are more likely to do if you are slouching or lounging. Keep a smile on your face. As silly as that may sound since no one can see you anyway, smiling will make you feel enthusiastic and, in turn, you will project enthusiasm. Phones tend to muffle our voices a bit, so make sure you speak into the phone clearly and slowly. Just as you would on a regular interview, think about what you're going to say before you speak. Avoid "ums" and other verbal space fillers. Pause instead. And take advantage of an opportunity you might not have during an in-person interview—refer to your resume when necessary. You can also have a cheat sheet of things you want to be sure to bring up. Keep a notepad handy so you can jot things down.

Video Interviews

You won't wonder whether or not it's okay to wear your pajamas if your interview is taking place via video. The interviewer will be able to see what you're wearing and doing; of course you have to look and act professionally. Follow all the general dress rules for in-person interviews. Wear a suit unless some other type of attire is more appropriate for that particular place of employment. Your hair should be nicely styled and your nails well groomed. Women's makeup should be kept simple.

As soon as you learn your interview is going to take place by video, find out what chat software the employer uses. Most likely it's Skype. You will have to sign up for a free account and then download the program from their website (*www.skype.com*). When you register, choose a professional-sounding user name like your full name or your first initial and last name. If you already have an account with a user name that doesn't sound professional enough, sign up for a second one. If you haven't video chatted before or if you haven't used the particular program the employer specified, a test run is definitely in order before your interview. After you install the software, make sure you know how to operate it and confirm that you know how your camera works. Then practice by video chatting with friends. Take this opportunity to have someone run through a mock interview with you, but now you can do it by video!

You must be in a completely quiet room as you would be for a phone interview. There's one big difference, however. Since the interviewer can see you, he can also see the room you're in. Make sure it's tidy and clean. Lock the door if you can, or issue a stern warning to anyone who might consider quietly tiptoeing through the room. Imagine that sight in the background!

Disable any alerts that could pop up on your computer screen as well as make noise. And never, ever check e-mail or anything else while you are in the middle of an interview; the interviewer will be able to see your hands on the keyboard. Turn off all phones and anything else that makes noise or that you may be tempted to steal a glance at.

During your video interview, sit up straight and not too close to the screen. Smile. Look at the camera in order to maintain good eye contact with your interviewer. Remember that looking into her eyes on your computer screen won't serve that purpose. Keep your hands lightly folded on the desk in front of you or on your lap. Since the microphone will pick up all extraneous noise, avoid tapping your feet, grinding your teeth, or shuffling through papers. While you are on camera, don't do anything you wouldn't do on an in-person interview. For example, don't stretch, get up, yawn, or blow your nose.

Group and Panel Interviews

At some point during your job search, you may have to participate in a group interview. In a group interview, several candidates are interviewed at one time. This type of interview allows those who are natural leaders to show themselves, and its purpose is often to find out who stands out from the crowd or emerges as a leader. If you aren't a leader, don't worry—not everyone can be one. The job may not be the right one for you. Trying to be someone you are not will only make things difficult down the line, when you or your employer discover you're not the right fit for the job after all. Whether you aren't or are a leader, make sure to speak up. Don't sit idly by while someone else does all the talking, but try not to interrupt participants.

When you walk into an interview, if you find yourself sitting at a table opposite several people, don't be alarmed. You are about to take part in a panel interview. This type of interview is also known as a committee interview, and is often used when a group of people must collectively decide whom to hire. During a panel interview, each member of the panel will ask you questions. The best thing you can do in this situation is to stay calm and answer the questions one at a time.

 Essential

During a panel interview, several people may be firing questions at once. Listen carefully, but if you don't hear the question, politely ask the person who asked it to repeat herself. When you answer questions during a panel interview, directly address the person who asked the question by making eye contact with her.

Interviewing over a Meal

When you find out your interview is going to take place over a meal, you may get indigestion before you even begin to eat. It is not enough to have to worry about impressing a potential employer with your words and avoiding any revealing body language; now you also have to worry about using the right fork, not spilling soup on yourself, and not having food stuck between your teeth. Here are some tips that will help you survive such an interview.

Sitting Down at the Table

When you arrive at the table, wait for everyone to sit down before you do, unless of course someone signals you to sit down first. After you sit down at the table, you should place your napkin on your lap. Generally you want to wait for your host to do this first. If the napkin is a large dinner-style one, you should fold it in half. If it is a small luncheon-style napkin, you can unfold it completely.

There may be a basket of bread on the table. If it is in front of you, offer it to your dining companions before you help yourself.

If it is not in front of you, wait until others have helped themselves before you ask someone to pass it to you. Do not reach in front of anyone or across the table to get it.

Fact

Place settings will often include a variety of utensils. Many people are confused about what to use first, second, and so forth. The rule of thumb is to start furthest away from your plate and work your way in as the meal progresses.

Place bread on your bread plate, which should be the smallest plate at your setting. Use your butter knife, or your regular knife if you do not have a butter knife, to place a piece of butter on your bread plate. Then break off a bite-size piece of bread, apply the butter to it, and eat that piece. Do not butter an entire slice of bread or roll at once and proceed to eat it like a sandwich.

What to Order

When the waitress arrives to take drink orders, make yours a soda or water. While an alcoholic beverage may calm you down, it may also loosen you up—too much. If your host orders a bottle of wine for the table, refusing to have some may appear rude. In that case, allow the waiter to pour some for you, but sip it slowly.

When it comes time to order your meal, choose wisely. Stay away from messy foods. Spaghetti is out, and avoid foods that tend to get stuck in your teeth, like spinach or poppy seeds. Choose something that is moderately priced. Your prospective employer is footing the bill, and you do not want to look greedy.

The Meal

When the food begins to arrive, wait until everyone is served before you begin eating. When you cut up your food, use both your knife and fork to cut off one piece at a time. Do not hold your knife in your hand while you are eating, and do not put a used utensil down on the table. Place your knife on your plate until you are ready to use it again.

 Essential

Carry a travel-size toothbrush and toothpaste or some dental floss with you to use after you eat. Go to the restroom to remove any food you fear is lodged between your teeth.

Use your napkin to remove any crumbs from your face. Remember to dab and not wipe. When you are done eating, place your napkin on the table. It should be folded neatly, not crumpled up. Then politely wait for everyone else to finish.

Don't Talk with Your Mouth Full

With your table manners in order, you can begin dealing with questions. The biggest one on your mind may be "How do I eat and answer questions at the same time?" With the finesse of a dentist, your interviewer may have a knack for asking you questions just as you put each forkful of food into your mouth. No matter how much you want to answer his questions, remember what your mom told you—don't talk with your mouth full. It only takes a few seconds to chew and swallow, although it may seem like an eternity to you. Remember to completely answer each question before you continue to eat.

Finishing Up

When your host places her napkin on the table, it signals that the meal is over. You do not want to keep her there any longer than necessary. This may or may not mean the end of the interview. Follow the interviewer's lead. When the interview is over, do what you would do at the end of a regular interview, with the addition of thanking her for the meal.

Interviewing in a Foreign Country

In today's global marketplace, it is possible that you could wind up interviewing for a job in a foreign country. If this happens, you will have to learn about the culture of that country, since a breach of etiquette could be interpreted as rudeness. You will have to learn about things like the proper way to greet someone, whether it is appropriate to look someone in the eye, and good table manners. The following guidelines will get you started.

Be sure you know the proper method of greeting in the country you are visiting. In some cultures people bow when they meet, but to complicate matters, different bows mean different things. You should make a point of learning the meaning of each one in order to avoid any missteps.

Certain body language, while acceptable in one culture, may be considered rude in another. For example, it is considered rude to look someone directly in the eye in some countries. What is appropriate for men in a particular culture may be inappropriate for women.

If you are interviewing in another country, it is very likely that you will be faced with an interview over a meal. You may be served unfamiliar foods, some of which you may not like or may not be accustomed to. When torn between being polite and being nauseated, it is okay not to eat something you find repulsive. You should accept what is offered; just don't put it in your mouth. You should also become acquainted with the table manners that are appropriate in that culture.

CHAPTER 5

Revealing Your Personality

You've met the interviewer, shaken his hand, and now you're settling into your seat. Okay, bring it on. You're ready for anything he's going to ask. You can talk about each job you've had, your skills, and your accomplishments. Suddenly you find yourself fielding a barrage of personal questions. The interviewer is asking about things that seem to have nothing to do with work. Why does he need to know so much about you?

Why the Personal Questions?

Why would an employer want to know what you like doing for fun, your strengths and weaknesses, and even how many siblings you grew up with? Or the most dreaded request: "So, tell me about yourself." Your heart begins to pound so loudly you're sure the interviewer can hear it. "Tell you about myself? Have you got a few hours?"

Be assured the interviewer usually doesn't want to know all the private details of your life. As a matter of fact, he doesn't have the right to ask for that kind of information. What a prospective employer is interested in learning about are your personal qualities, or your character traits. This information will help him decide whether to hire you.

Basically, the prospective employer wants to know if you have what it takes to work at his company. Yes, you may have the skills and experience, but do you have the personality? Aspects of your personality are strong indicators of whether you will be a good employee. The interviewer wants to know whether or not you procrastinate, are discreet, and are a team player. He wants to know if you work well on your own and how you make decisions, handle stress, and solve problems.

Before beginning the interviewing process, a hiring manager may have gone through hundreds of resumes looking for candidates who have the skills and experience required for the job in question. The interviewer's job now is to be a detective. He wants to know what makes you a better choice than another candidate who has the same experience and skills.

 Alert

Don't reveal more about yourself than is necessary during a job interview. While you should be honest with the interviewer, don't tell her more than she needs to know. Revealing too much can get you into trouble.

An interviewer will try to learn about your personality by asking you either direct questions (e.g., "Do you tend to begin a project as soon as it is assigned, or do you begin working as you get close to the deadline?") or by asking you questions that get you to reveal this information (e.g., "Tell me how you approach a new project"). Give careful consideration to every question the interviewer asks. He has a reason for each one of them, and figuring out what it is can help you give the best answer.

Now, let's get back to the dreaded question: "Tell me about yourself." The interviewer doesn't want your memoirs. The rule of thumb is to keep it simple. The interviewer is interested only in knowing whether you have the skills and qualities necessary to fulfill the job requirements. Interviewees sometimes make the mistake of revealing too much when what the prospective employer really wants to know is "Can you do the job?" and "Will you fit in here?"

Questions and Answers

Q Tell me about yourself.

A I attended Ace Business College, where I earned my associate's degree in office technology five years ago. I started working as a library clerk right after I graduated, and I was promoted to assistant circulation manager after a year. I helped the library switch over to a new circulation system about two years ago. I was part of the team that selected the new system and I helped train our department in its use. In addition to my technical skills, I am adept at troubleshooting. I also work well with customers, helping to solve any problems that arise. I'm now ready to take on a job with more responsibility, and I know I will make a great circulation manager.

This candidate tells the interviewer about his skills and experience and shows why he is qualified for the job. He doesn't wander off course or reveal information that is irrelevant. Although this answer is a bit long, it is to the point and tells the interviewer only what she needs to know.

Never Say: "I was born in Wisconsin, one of three children. I did well in school. I was on the football team and editor of my high school newspaper. I moved to Chicago to go to college and . . ." The interviewer doesn't want your life story. Keep your answer limited to the parts that will affect your suitability for the job.

Q Do you work well on your own?

A Yes, I do. I'm very focused and efficient.

This is a very simple and honest answer. Most jobs will require you to work on your own sometimes, if not all the time.

Never Say: "I would much rather work on my own." In addition to sometimes working on your own, many jobs also require you to be part of a team at times. Don't volunteer information that makes you seem difficult to work with; just answer the question.

Q What do you consider to be your biggest weakness?

A I am very dedicated to my job, and I expect the same level of dedication from other people. Not everyone feels the same way about work, and sometimes my expectations are too high.

Wouldn't every boss love such a dedicated employee? This interviewee knew he had to find a weakness that his prospective employer would see as a strength.

Never Say: "I don't have any weaknesses." Oh, come on. Who's going to believe that?

Q What would your friends say is your biggest weakness?

A Whenever my friends and I travel together, I do a lot of advanced planning. Most of my travel companions appreciate it, but some find it annoying. We just went to the Southwest, and three months before we were going I had already put together a list of all the things we had to see. I kept everyone going all day long, every single day. In the end we all had a great time.

This candidate chooses to talk about something that could be perceived as a weakness but that also demonstrates her skills. By giving this answer, she demonstrates three skills—planning, research, and strong leadership qualities. Some of her friends may not appreciate her advanced planning, which is why she considers this a weakness, but she also shows that everything worked out in the end.

Never Say: "I never see my friends because I'm always working." You know what they say about all work and no play. A little time away from the office is good for everyone.

Q How do you handle success?

A I give myself a quick pat on the back and move on to the next project. Of course, I take the time to figure out what helped me succeed and use that experience to help me the next time.

This prospective employee takes appropriate pride in his success but also believes in the old adage "Don't rest on your laurels." He also learns from his experience.

Never Say: "I make sure everyone knows about it. If I don't brag about my own success, then who will?" That's true, but there are more subtle ways of getting the word out. Besides, if he's so busy bragging, who's doing all his work?

Q How do you handle failure?

A I give myself a short time to feel sad, but I don't dwell on it. Who has time for that? I don't spend too much energy on my failures, but I always try to figure out where things went wrong. If I don't do that, I won't know what I need to do to succeed next time.

This isn't someone who wastes any time feeling sorry for herself. She's also smart enough to learn from her mistakes.

Never Say: "I never fail, so I don't have to handle it." Everyone has failures, so the interviewer can only assume this candidate is lying or joking. Either way, she may be able to count this interview among her failures.

Q What are your long-term goals?

A I want to move into a supervisory position eventually. I know that will take time and hard work, but it is something I expect to achieve.

That's a good answer as long as the applicant isn't implying that he wants the interviewer's job. Making the interviewer feel threatened will not win him any points. It's important to emphasize not only that you have goals, but also that you are willing to do the work to reach them.

Never Say: "I want to run this place." Wait. Doesn't the interviewer run this place?

Q What are your short-term goals?

A I want to work for a growing company in a position that allows me to use my skills to help that growth. I know your company is trying to expand into the teen market. My experience selling to that market will help your company reach its goals.

This interviewee's goals are aligned with those of the company. By giving an example of how she will help the company meet its goals, she has forced the employer to visualize her as an employee. This answer also shows that the interviewee took the time to research the company before her appointment.

Never Say: "I plan to begin working on my MBA as soon as possible." While this interviewee is clearly ambitious, she hasn't shown how her goals have anything to do with the job for which she's interviewing.

Q Do you prefer to work alone or as part of a team?

A Each situation is different. When I'm working on some projects, I prefer to be part of a team, while I'd rather work alone on other projects. I enjoy being part of a team, but I can work independently, too.

This interviewer shows that he's flexible and can adapt to working in either situation.

Never Say: "Teams are clearly a better use of resources. I'm a team player all the way." It's important to show flexibility, because most jobs require you to be able to work independently at least some of the time as well as on a team.

Q What do you consider to be your greatest strength?

A My greatest strength is my ability to see a project through from its inception to its completion. Each project I am assigned is important to me, and I always make sure it gets the appropriate amount of attention.

Notice the interviewee said each project gets the "appropriate amount of attention" and not "all my attention." She clearly knows some projects need more attention than others and indicates that she knows how to prioritize.

Never Say: "I'm a hard worker and I always get to work on time." Getting to work on time is expected of all workers, as is being a hard worker. These are requirements of most jobs, not strengths.

Q How many siblings did you grow up with, and how did that influence who you are today?

A *Answer 1:* I grew up as one of five children. When you grow up in such a large family, you must function as a team. Everyone takes on different responsibilities. Because my parents were so busy all the time, I also learned to be very independent.

A *Answer 2:* I grew up as an only child, so I was very independent. When I got to school, I had to learn how to share my toys with other kids. It was a difficult lesson that helped me become a better team player.

The interviewee, regardless of the size family in which he grew up, shows that he can work alone or as part of a team.

Never Say: Answer 1: "I grew up with five brothers and sisters. It was always really noisy. I think that's why I love being alone now."

Never Say: Answer 2: "I was an only child. I got so used to being alone that I really like it better that way." Uh oh. Neither answer shows that the interviewee is flexible enough to be a team player when he needs to be.

Q Do you like to take risks or are you cautious?

A I'll take risks but I always proceed with caution, so I guess I fall somewhere in between. I like to see what my odds are before I take a risk. I also want to know what I stand to gain or what I stand to lose.

This candidate is a careful decision-maker who isn't afraid to take risks if there is a high probability of success. She also wants to make sure the risk is worth taking. She's not a gambler, but she's not afraid to take chances when it's appropriate to do so.

Never Say: "I'm a risk-taker" or "I'm cautious." Most employers want someone with a combination of these traits.

Q Do others think of you as a leader?

A I believe those who have seen me in action are confident in my ability to lead them. Whenever we had to work in committees in my marketing class, my fellow committee members always chose me to be chairperson.

This answer is honest and to the point. Although he is interviewing for his first job, he is able to draw on his college experience to come up with an example.

Never Say: "I lead and others follow." Confidence is good, but cockiness is not.

Q Do you consider yourself a leader?

A I am willing to take on responsibility, I am persuasive, and I can delegate. All these qualities make me a good leader. If a situation calls for someone to take charge, I will certainly step forward.

This interviewee states the qualities that make her a good leader but knows to tread lightly here. She wants to show she can evalu-

ate the needs of each situation and step forward if necessary, while making it clear she's a team player.

Never Say: "Yes. I like being in charge." This candidate doesn't tell the interviewer why she is qualified to lead, but sounds determined to take a leadership position no matter whom she steps on.

 Alert

> Make sure to fully answer the interviewer's question. Explain yourself clearly and don't give answers that are too short, but also avoid ones that are too lengthy. Try to figure out why the interviewer has asked a particular question, and prepare your answer with that in mind.

Q How do you handle pressure?

A I take a deep breath and figure out what needs to be done. Then I take care of it. One afternoon at 4 P.M., my boss came to me with a big research project that needed to be completed by the following morning. I rounded up my team and divided the project among us. We got it done with enough time to get home to sleep for a few hours before returning to work in the morning.

This interviewee has a strategy in place for dealing with pressure. He demonstrates how he dealt with one difficult situation using some valuable skills, including the abilities to delegate and work as part of a team.

Never Say: "I work best under pressure." That may be true, but this interviewee needs to elaborate.

Q Are you a procrastinator, or do you like to get things done right away?

A Though I've been known to procrastinate on occasion, I don't make a habit of it. When someone hands me a project that needs to be done in a timely fashion, I will get it done.

Who hasn't procrastinated on occasion? What matters is that this candidate knows the difference between a project that can wait and one that needs to be done right away, and can finish the pressing ones in time to meet deadlines.

Never Say: "I never procrastinate." Really? This doesn't sound like an honest answer, since everyone procrastinates at least some of the time. Everyone has flaws. Your goal on a job interview is to make yours not look so bad.

Q What pet peeves do you have about coworkers?

A Too much negativity has always bothered me. I think if you're going to complain, you should be able to offer some solutions to fix the things you think are wrong.

By giving this answer, this candidate is saying, "I'm not a negative person. If I see a problem, I figure out how to fix it."

Never Say: "I say live and let live. They can do what they want; it doesn't bother me." It's virtually impossible to spend forty hours a week with a group of people and get along perfectly with them all the time. This candidate seems to be too easygoing. She'd rather let things slide than deal with them.

Q We're not a company that does things the same way year after year. How do you react to change?

A When it's appropriate, change is important. For example, when I heard about a new payroll system at a conference last year, I did a little investigating, found out it was better than what we were using, and recommended my employer move over to it.

This interviewee has shown that he doesn't shy away from change and even provides a good example of how he initiated it at his current job. He has also shown that he doesn't jump into change just for the sake of doing something different; instead, he does his homework first.

Never Say: "Change is great. Without it I get bored." The interviewer might wonder if the candidate's love of change includes finding a new job every other year.

Q What is the last thing you read?

A I just finished the latest book on management techniques by Jane Brown. I'm always trying to keep up with the latest literature in the field.

Reading is a great way to keep up with changes in one's field and this interviewee knows it. She proves that her interest in the field goes beyond the nine-to-five job.

Never Say: "My job keeps me so busy I really don't have time to read." Even if you don't have time to read for pleasure, you should have time to keep up with your professional literature if you want to be seen as a dedicated applicant.

Question

Should I discuss my personal likes and dislikes on a job interview?
Only if you can relate them to your career or to the job for which you are interviewing. For example, if a prospective employer asks what you like to read, stick to talking about professional literature.

Q How do you make decisions?

A I evaluate the situation before I decide what I need to do. If there is someone who has had experience with similar situations, I'm not afraid to ask for advice.

This interviewee isn't going to make a decision without considering it carefully. She is also very resourceful; seeking advice from people with more experience is always a good idea.

Never Say: "I usually go with my first instinct." This interviewee clearly doesn't put a lot of thought into things, including how to best answer this question.

 Fact

Interviewers are generally quite perceptive, and therefore they will know when a job candidate is giving answers that are too good to be true. It is important to frame your answers so they are as positive as possible, but don't go over the top. Keep your answers realistic.

Q I see that you worked full time while attending graduate school. How did you manage to balance everything?

A It was difficult, but I managed not to fall behind at work or school. I worked five full days a week and took classes two evenings a week. I studied on the other three nights and on the weekends.

This candidate shows that she was determined to complete her degree, but not at the expense of her job.

Never Say: "I walked around exhausted all the time." This doesn't answer the interviewer's question or tell him anything about the candidate other than that she doesn't handle stress well.

 Alert

Always pay attention and listen carefully during the interview. If you don't understand a question completely, it's okay to ask for clarification. It's better than answering incorrectly. You won't be able to answer a question properly unless you understand what the interviewer is asking you.

Q Can you describe your ideal work environment?

A I want to work in an environment where I can use my presentation skills to help the company increase its client roster. It's important that I work in a fast-paced environment, because I like being busy. I want to work somewhere where employees are recognized for their contributions.

Based on some research, this candidate is able to describe both the job that she's interviewing for and her potential employer. By showing that her ideal fits with what the job requires, she shows that she is the perfect fit for the position.

Never Say: "I want to work in a clean office with good lighting. I prefer to be on a lower floor. I really don't like cubicles." Even if this candidate had done her homework, and this was an accurate description of her potential employer's offices, this answer doesn't say anything about the job or her qualifications for it.

Q Why did you choose this career?

A When I started college, I wasn't sure what I wanted to do. I visited the career office and they gave me some self-assessment tests. Based on the results, they gave me a list of careers that might be suitable and told me how to research them. I did, and this is what I thought I'd like best.

This is a great answer that demonstrates this candidate's ability to go about making life-altering decisions in a methodical fashion.

Never Say: "My parents had a friend in the field and she thought I'd be good at this." That is the wrong way to make a career choice. It may make the interviewer wonder how this person will make other decisions.

CHAPTER 6

Discussing Your Skills and Abilities

Your skills—that's what they pay you the big bucks for. Well, maybe not the big bucks, but it is why they pay you anything at all. Who you are as a person will help an employer decide if you have the characteristics that make you a good fit for his company. To fit into a particular job, you'll also need a certain set of skills. Your skills represent your ability to do the job at hand.

Hard Skills versus Soft Skills

Skills can be divided into two categories: hard skills and soft skills. Hard skills are the technical skills that define your job. Soft skills are less tangible. They begin with how you present yourself in your first encounter with your prospective employer, whether it is an in-person or remote interview. Your prospective employer will want to know that you will fit into the work environment at her company and be able to handle the demands that will be placed upon you.

Hard Skills

Simply put, a baker must know how to bake, an accountant must know how to balance the books, a nurse must know how to care for patients, and a teacher must know how to teach. Of course, these basic skills can be broken down into more specific hard skills. For example, an accountant might be skilled in particular areas—specifically, accounts receivable, accounts payable, auditing, taxation, and payroll.

 Fact

Hard skills are usually skills you learned in school or through some other formal training or prior work experience. You will typically choose a job based on the hard skills you possess, but some employers are willing to let you pick them up on the job.

What you do at work can vary greatly from your formal job description. In addition to your regular job duties, you may be required to write, make presentations, use a computer, or do research. These are also hard skills, but they are not necessarily part of your "official" job description. Nevertheless, you will be required to be proficient in these skills and your prospective employer will want you to prove this in your interview by drawing on specific examples of how you have used your skills.

Soft Skills

Soft skills are the skills you must have in order to excel at work in general. These skills vary greatly. They aren't specific to any occupation, but instead are the things that enhance your performance regardless of what your actual job is. Examples of these soft skills include decision making, time management, delegating, multitasking, and problem solving.

Remember, when the job interviewer asks whether you have a particular skill, she doesn't want a simple yes or no answer. She wants to know how you obtained the skill, how you've used the skill, and how you plan to use it to benefit her company.

Essential

When you prepare for a job interview, make a list of all your soft skills and all your hard skills. Think of specific examples of when you've had to use each of them, especially those that are most relevant to the job for which you are interviewing.

Skills You Haven't Used Professionally

You may be concerned if you have a particular skill, but you haven't actually used it on the job. You may have learned it in school and never used it at work. If this is the case, can you think of a time you used that skill for an extracurricular activity or in another situation? Perhaps you used your fundraising skills to raise money for an organization for which you volunteer or your organizational skills to plan an event.

 Fact

People develop skills in a variety of ways that are unrelated to paid employment. You may have learned a new skill when you participated in a school club or organization. You may use certain skills in running your household or in your volunteer work.

When discussing skills you've picked up through volunteer work or some other unpaid experience, talk about the skill as if you've used it on a job. Highlight how your skills benefited the organization or club. For example, if you raised funds, give dollar amounts; if you organized an event, state how many people attended it. If you haven't actually used a skill in a real-life situation, you can still lay claim to it. Come up with an example of how you would use it to benefit your prospective employer.

Questions and Answers

Q How well do you think you perform as a manager?

A I've never officially had the title "manager," but I've often had to act as manager when my boss was out of the office. He's always been very pleased with the job I've done.

This candidate doesn't let the fact that she's never actually had the title of manager stop her from explaining why she can do the job. She found some managerial experience from which she was able to draw. Even supervising a small project would have sufficed.

Never Say: "Well, since I've never been a manager, I don't know." If you've had some managerial experience, even if it was just supervising a single project, you should talk about that. If you've had no managerial experience, then you can talk about it hypothetically.

Q How are your presentation skills? How do you prepare for presentations?

A I didn't always like making presentations, but since I had to make a lot of them in my last two jobs, I've gotten very good at it. I do a lot of research before any presentation. I try to find out as much as possible about the client, the market they are trying to reach, their competitors, and the industry. Sometimes, if the budget allows for it, I hire an expert to help me with the research.

This candidate answered honestly. He knows it's not that unusual to dislike presentations, so he's not afraid to admit that. It also gives him the opportunity to show off his experience and explain how it has gotten him over his fear. In addition, he knows the importance of having good information and knows what resources he needs to use to get it.

Never Say: "I love making presentations. I only have one real problem; if I'm too prepared, my presentation sounds scripted."

This is not a well-thought-out answer. This candidate would have benefited from a little preparation to get him through the interview.

Q You haven't worked in this field before. What makes you think you'd be good at this?

A I am very organized, I work well on a team, and I have very good communication skills. Although I haven't worked in this particular field before, I know these skills will make me a valuable employee.

This applicant doesn't let the fact that she's new to this field stop her from showing the interviewer why he should hire her. She has some very desirable skills for this and any field, which she makes a point of letting the interviewer know.

Never Say: "I haven't worked in this field before, but I'm a fast learner." This candidate makes the mistake of dwelling on her lack of experience in this particular field instead of on her strengths.

Q Have you ever been in a situation where the majority disagrees with you? What did you do?

A I haven't been in that situation, but here's what I would do if I were: First I would listen to why the majority felt the way they did. Then I'd decide whether I needed to reconsider my position. If I still felt strongly about it after hearing their side, I would try to persuade them to come over to mine.

This candidate knew better than to dismiss the question just because he couldn't draw on his experience to answer it. Rather than make something up, he tells the interviewer what he would do if he were in that situation. His answer shows that he is flexible enough to try to see things differently, but strong enough in his convictions to not automatically go with the crowd.

Never Say: "We were designing our new brochure and I thought yellow and purple would look great. Everyone else wanted to go with burgundy and blue. Since I had the most seniority, they had to do it my way." Flexible? No. A bully? Maybe.

Q Please describe your work in the military.

A As an Army finance specialist, I audited financial records, disbursed cash and checks, and recorded details of financial transactions using standard forms.

This job candidate, an Army veteran, clearly states what her military work involved. Since military job descriptions are often different from civilian job descriptions, it was not only important for her to state what her title was, but to also describe her duties.

Never Say: "I was a finance specialist." This isn't descriptive enough, particularly since the title may differ from the actual job description.

Q How are you at delegating?

A I have such a high level of trust in my staff members that delegating to them is easy. I know each person's strengths and weaknesses, so I can easily decide who can handle certain jobs and duties. I try to give people projects that challenge them but won't defeat them.

This candidate is obviously a good manager. He puts a lot of thought into how to delegate responsibilities and makes a point of knowing his staff very well.

Never Say: "I'm good at delegating. I don't want to do all the work myself." This guy just sounds lazy.

Q Tell me about a crisis you encountered at work and how you handled it.

A Last year, a virus was causing our computers to send out thousands of e-mail messages to our clients. We were being inundated with angry phone calls before we even knew what was going on. Our technical support person was on vacation, so I made a few phone calls and found someone to fix the problem. Then, once she removed the virus from our system, I drafted an apology that was sent out by e-mail to our clients.

This answer is good because the candidate clearly describes the problem and gives specifics on how he solved it. In addition, the crisis is one that could have caused his company to lose clients, something that would strike fear into the hearts of most employers, including the one interviewing him.

Never Say: "My assistant called in sick right before I was leaving on vacation. I was counting on her to run some errands for me. Since she wasn't there, I had to get one of the interns to do it." This candidate is resourceful, but he shouldn't have had anyone running his errands on company time.

Q How do you manage your time?

A I prioritize my work. I figure out what needs to get done first, next, and so on. Then I calculate how much time I will need to spend on each activity or project. I set a schedule for myself and get going.

This applicant has a plan. He knows how to prioritize and apportion the proper amount of time to each activity.

Never Say: "I get to work early and stay late to get everything done." This answer doesn't show that the applicant can manage his time well. Rather, he can get everything done as long as he works long hours, which could cost the employer in overtime.

Q How do you solve problems?

A First I assess the problem. Then I figure out what I need to do to solve it. For example, last month we were hosting a conference. Our receptionist, who was supposed to greet attendees, called in sick. With the conference scheduled to start in an hour, we had to do something fast. I quickly went through a list of employees who might be able to handle hosting duties but found that each was involved in some other aspect of the conference. I got my boss's approval to call my contact at a local temp agency, and we had a replacement host shortly.

Not only does this applicant discuss how she solves problems, she gives a real-life example.

Never Say: "If you do your job well, you shouldn't have any problems to solve." This candidate is in a state of denial. Problems always pop up, and she has shown that she will have no idea how to deal with them when they do.

Q We use PQR Write to lay out our brochures. Do you know how to use it?

A I use a program that is very similar to that. I also have a friend who uses PQR, and I'm sure she'd be happy to give me a crash course. I know I can learn it by the time I start work.

There are so many software programs out there, it would be impossible to know how to use all of them. This candidate knew better than to lie about his experience and instead told his prospective employer how he would get the skills he needs. Notice how he says he'll know the program by the time "I start work," not "if I get this job."

Never Say: "No, I only feel comfortable with Super Page. Couldn't I just keep using that?"

Q Are you computer literate?

A I'm proficient in several programs, including WordRight, Bottom Line, and Quick Pages.

Instead of just saying she is computer literate, this candidate goes beyond that and discusses which software programs she knows how to use. The programs she chooses to highlight are those that are relevant to the job for which she's applying.

Never Say: "I know how to go online and I can use a word processor." This candidate should be more specific, making a point of mentioning programs that are specific to his field.

Q We handle a large volume of tax returns here. How has your experience prepared you for this?

A During college, I participated in the IRS's Volunteer Income Tax Assistance program. For two nights a week from February through April, I spent a few hours preparing individual tax returns in a public library near my college. I prepared about five returns each evening.

This job candidate, although he doesn't have professional experience, is able to demonstrate his skills through his volunteer experience. He speaks about the number of tax returns he processed, demonstrating that he can work efficiently.

Never Say: "I do a few returns each year, but I'm sure I'll be able to handle the volume." Even if this candidate can't demonstrate that he has practical experience preparing a large volume of tax returns, he should find some past experience that proves to the interviewer he can handle a large volume of work.

Q Have you ever had to juggle two or more projects at the same time?

A That happened all the time on my last job. Several months ago, I was in the midst of working on one huge project for one of my bosses, when my other boss came to me with another project that needed to be completed in two days. After evaluating the second project, I realized I could complete it in one day. Since I still had about a week before the deadline for the first project, I decided to get started on the second one. I completed it by the end of the next day and went back to my first project.

The interviewer asked for an example and this candidate gave one. She demonstrates how her ability to prioritize helped her.

Never Say: "I can't think of any right now. Can I get back to you on that one?" The interviewee should have prepared for this in advance.

Q We need someone with very strong auditing skills. Do you qualify?

A Yes, I do. As a staff accountant at Crabgrass and Weed, I regularly performed audits of our clients' financial records. I examined financial source documents to make sure procedures were followed correctly and generated adjusting journal entries as needed. I also prepared final reports for our clients.

The interviewee specifically states how her experience has prepared her for this position.

Never Say: "Yes, I do. I had some auditing responsibilities on my last job." This applicant has the necessary skills, but she needs to elaborate on them.

Q How do you take direction?

A I think the ability to listen is one of the most important skills anyone should have. I always make sure to pay attention to what my supervisor is saying and then ask any questions I have. I find out when the project must be completed and if there are any special issues I must be attentive to.

This candidate demonstrates that he has no problem taking direction from his superiors, or for that matter, following those directions.

Never Say: "Why should that matter? Won't I be in charge?" Even if this person is applying for a high-level position, he will still have to answer to someone, unless he plans to buy the company.

Q As assistant to the director of human resources, employees will come to you if they feel their supervisor has discriminated against them in some way. How will you handle these complaints?

A As an HR professional, I know the importance of being well versed in the laws that affect the workplace. First I will interview the employee, asking for an explanation of exactly what happened. Then I'll interview the supervisor and get her side of the story.

This candidate will take a balanced look at the situation. He will evaluate it using his knowledge of employment law and then try to solve the problem.

Never Say: "I'd refer it to our company's legal counsel." This applicant needs to show he knows how to deal with issues that regularly occur before dumping them in someone else's lap.

Q What skills can you bring to our school?

A As you can see from my resume, I've been a teacher at the Parkside School for five years. I've taught second and third grades. I form strong relationships with my students. They trust me, as do their parents. Many view me as a strict teacher, and in fact, I am an excellent classroom manager. My students know what I expect of them and are generally very cooperative. I am a skilled communicator, and I structure my lessons so that I reach all my students. My classes always perform well on statewide exams.

This applicant knows what skills make a successful teacher and she has shown that she possesses them all.

Never Say: "I love kids and I'm a good teacher." This candidate needs to do more than state the obvious.

Q As principal, the most frequent complaint I hear from parents is about teachers who don't maintain good communications with them. What have you done as a teacher to help maintain communication with parents of your students?

A First of all, parents can reach me by e-mail, by sending in a note, or by telephone. If I am not able to respond immediately, I always get back to them before the end of the day. I encourage parents to come to the classroom to read to the children. I send home a "Dear Parents" letter every two weeks, explaining what we've covered in the classroom during the prior two weeks and what we will be covering during the upcoming weeks.

This job candidate talks about what he is currently doing to maintain good communications with parents. Not only does he communicate with parents when he has an issue to discuss, he also keeps the lines of communication open.

Never Say: "When there's a problem, I contact the parents immediately." The principal wants to know how this teacher communicates regularly, not only if there's something that needs to be discussed.

Q You have many of the skills we're looking for. However, we also need someone with very strong sales skills. I don't see anything on your resume that indicates you have that kind of experience.

A Yes, it's true that I don't have any formal experience in sales. I do have some informal experience, however. I ran the book fair at my son's school for the past few years and raised $3,000. I also sold jewelry that a friend made. We rented tables at craft fairs all over the region and sold about twenty pieces at each one. Even after covering the price of the table and supplies and paying me, she made a decent profit.

While a candidate can't make up experience, he should draw on unpaid or volunteer experience that demonstrates his skills. He gives very specific examples.

Never Say: "No, I don't have any sales experience, but I can learn." This candidate should try to find some past experience that demonstrates his skills. If he truly has no sales experience, he might consider the qualities that make a good salesperson and find a way to demonstrate that he has those qualities.

Q We expect the executive director to handle a lot of fundraising. Do you have any experience with that?

A Yes, I do. I spearheaded a campaign that raised more than $10,000 for a small library for our members. I also run an annual campaign to raise money for our after-school center. Over the last five years, we've increased donations by about 6 percent each year.

This candidate quantifies her accomplishments. It's one way of saying "here's what I did for my current employer and this is what I can do for you."

Never Say: "I've done some fundraising on my job." This candidate needs to be more specific.

Q What is your management style?

A I'm a hands-on manager. I dive right in and work alongside my employees. This not only sets a good example for them, but also helps keep me aware of everyone's strengths and weaknesses.

This interviewee knows how to keep people motivated. She provides a reason for having chosen that style.

Never Say: "I'm very strict. I say how and when things get done." Ruling with an iron fist does not lead to a satisfied staff.

Q Are you good at doing research?

A I haven't done a great deal of research at work, but I do a lot of it on my own. Before I make any major purchases, take any medication, or go on vacation, I do a lot of research. I'm very good at it. The librarians at my local library are a great resource, so I make sure to go to them when I need help.

It would have been nice if this job candidate could have drawn on work experience to highlight his research skills, but since he couldn't, he did the next best thing. He gave examples of what kind of research he has done and explains how he does it.

Never Say: "I guess so. I like using the Net." An avid Internet user does not necessarily make a good researcher.

Q As you know, this is a new programming-director position. We're thinking about having the person in this position also handle promoting our programs. Is that something you can handle?

A My primary responsibility as program director at the Art Council was program development. However, we had a very small staff, so I was usually responsible for promotion as well. I wrote press releases, designed print ads, and compiled mailing lists. This would be a great way to utilize my skills.

While highlighting her primary skill, program development, this applicant also draws upon some of her secondary responsibilities to explain why this job is a good fit.

Never Say: "I would be thrilled to be doing publicity. That was my favorite part of my last job." The interviewer said that publicity might be part of this job. If it turned out not to be, would this candidate be disappointed and quit?

Q How do you think others rate you as a supervisor?

A Turnover in my department since I was promoted to supervisor five years ago has decreased from 30 percent to 10 percent. The reason, I believe, is that I treat those who work under me fairly. When a big deadline is coming up, I'm right there working late with them and not heading out the door at 5 P.M. I've had employees tell me they appreciate that.

This candidate knows that saying he's highly regarded as a supervisor isn't enough. He needs to back up his claim, which he does by telling his prospective employer how much turnover in his department decreased since he's been there. He goes on to tell the interviewer why he believes this is so.

Never Say: "They think I'm a good supervisor. They never complain and they do what I tell them to do." There's more to being a good supervisor than this.

Q I see from your resume this isn't your first job working in a medical office. What skills did you pick up on your two previous jobs that you think would help you on this job?

A When you described the job to me, you said you needed someone who was good with patients. You also said you wanted someone who knows a lot about the different insurance plans. My primary responsibility at both these jobs was billing. I had to deal with insurance companies every day. I found that if I learned how each one worked, it was a lot easier for the doctors in my practice to get paid and for patients to get reimbursed. I also worked at the reception desk at these jobs. Many patients who came in were clearly anxious. I was happy to be able to calm them down and hopefully offer some reassurance.

This candidate listened to what the employer said and was able to clearly state how her skills would fill this medical practice's needs.

Never Say: "You wanted someone who is good with patients and insurance. That would be me." This candidate needs to elaborate.

Q Please discuss a project you supervised.

A I managed the expansion project at the shopping mall in Greenhaven. It involved increasing the size of the mall by 20 percent. I supervised a staff of fifty-five project team professionals. We completed the project within our budget.

By giving details about this project, including specific numbers, this interviewer demonstrates the type of work of which he's capable.

Never Say: "I supervised a mall expansion right outside the city. It went well." This answer is too vague.

Q What traits will a person need in order to become successful? Do you have these traits?

A To be successful, a person needs excellent organization and time management skills. She has to get along well with her boss, coworkers, and clients. She must always be willing to learn new skills. Yes, I have all these traits.

This interviewee has chosen to discuss some very valuable skills—organization, time management, willingness to learn, and getting along with others.

Never Say: "A person must be good at office politics. I've had lots of experience with that, and I'm very good at it." Knowing how to "play the game" may help you be successful, but your success may not be based on any real skills.

CHAPTER 7

Highlighting Your Accomplishments

When you go in for a job interview, the prospective employer will be very interested in learning about your accomplishments as well as your personality and skills. Your accomplishments give him insight into what you are capable of doing for him and his company. An accomplishment can be defined as something you've successfully achieved as a direct result of your efforts.

Listing Your Accomplishments

Prepare a list of your accomplishments prior to your job interview. Choose to highlight those that demonstrate your skills and abilities. Remember to use examples of things that came about as a direct result of your efforts. They shouldn't be things that happened to you, like raises or promotions, but rather things you made happen. That's not to say you shouldn't mention that your employer promoted you or rewarded you in another way because of something you accomplished—you should talk about that. Before you do, however, discuss the accomplishment that led to your reward and the role you played in making your accomplishment come about.

The accomplishments you include on your list should be realistic and verifiable. Never stretch the truth—not even a little bit—on a job interview. The interviewer might be suspicious if something sounds too good to be true and decide to check up on it. If she tries to verify something you told her and cannot, it will certainly reflect poorly on you. Lying is much worse than not having a long list of accomplishments.

When possible, quantify your accomplishments. Use actual numbers or percentages when you are discussing anything that can be expressed in quantifiable terms, such as increases in profits or decreases in costs. Being able to say you increased sales by 20 percent or cut your department's costs by 35 percent is much better than saying "I increased sales a lot" or "I cut costs greatly."

 Fact

> Consider keeping a career journal to record all of your achievements and the steps you took to achieve your goals. This will help you be specific on future job interviews. Listing accomplishments as they occur is easier than trying to think back and recall them.

When deciding which achievements to discuss on an interview, always remember to choose the ones that best demonstrate your ability to do the job for which you are interviewing. Highlight skills you think the prospective employer is looking for in a new employee.

Discussing Your Accomplishments

You will have many opportunities to talk about your accomplishments throughout a job interview. The prospective employer will, of course, ask you direct questions about your accomplishments. You can also impress the interviewer with additional accomplishments if you answer his questions about your skills by discussing how a particular skill helped you achieve something.

A prospective employer is likely to ask you questions about your goals, both work-related and personal. Your goals are merely accomplishments waiting to happen. Discuss goals you have already reached and those you are moving toward reaching. Talk about the steps you took, or are taking, to do so.

Alert

You may be asked about your personal goals as well as your professional ones. Even when discussing personal goals and achievements, make sure they highlight an ability related to work; for example, perseverance or organizational skills.

This is your time to brag about what you have done and what you can do. People are often quite hesitant to speak highly of themselves. They are under the impression that being boastful is obnoxious. This may, in fact, be true in our private lives. But the job interview is not the time for modesty. You must sell yourself, and to do so you have to show off.

Questions and Answers

Q Can you tell me about your greatest accomplishment at work?

A I'm particularly proud of the mentoring program I started about five years ago. I noticed that new employees were having trouble getting acclimated to the company, causing a very high turnover rate during the first year of employment. I developed a program that allowed us to assign each new employee to an employee who had been with the company for at least three years. This allowed new hires to make a smoother transition. Now, 90 percent of new employees are still with us after their one-year anniversaries, up from 50 percent before we started the mentorship program.

The interviewee provides a specific example in response to this question. She also highlights the fact that she took initiative in developing it—she saw a problem and found a solution. Notice that she uses actual numbers to illustrate the result of her efforts.

Never Say: "I was promoted to assistant director of human resources." While it is important to share this information, this interviewee doesn't indicate what led to that promotion.

Q How did you progress at your last job?

A I was hired as a sales associate by K.R. Nickel Stores seven years ago. I became assistant manager of the girls' clothing department two years later. My boss said she never saw a young associate work as hard as I did. After two more years, I was promoted to manager of that department.

This candidate simply describes his ascent up the corporate ladder, giving details as he was asked to do.

Never Say: "I started as a sales associate, and seven years later I'm manager of girls' clothing." This interviewee must talk about how he got from point A to point C.

Q How do you feel about the way your career has progressed so far?

A I'm pleased with how my career has progressed. When I graduated from college, I was hired to work as a trainee at Rogers, Inc., a small advertising agency. Being a trainee meant I answered the phones and made coffee. I took the initiative and asked for additional work. That gave me the opportunity to prove myself, and I was promoted to assistant account executive after eight months. After two years in that position, during which I worked on several successful ad campaigns, I was promoted to account executive. I'm proud of my work there, but it's time for a position with more responsibility.

This candidate takes the time to explain how her career has progressed since her graduation from college. She also makes sure to point out how she contributed to her firm's success.

Never Say: "I am very happy with it. I started off answering phones and now look where I am." Don't assume the interviewer knows where you are right now or how you got there.

Q Why do you think you've been successful in your career so far?

A I've been successful so far because I've always worked very hard and I've always been willing to accept any challenges that are offered to me. Actually, I usually seek them out. I have excellent time-management skills that have allowed me to complete projects on time.

This interviewee hasn't relied on luck to achieve success. He has used his skills and motivation to get where he wants to be.

Never Say: "I've always been in the right place at the right time." This candidate doesn't seem to think he had anything to do with his own success. If he doesn't believe it, who will?

Q Which of your accomplishments has given you the most satisfaction?

A Last year I initiated a program that sent our executives into schools to work with the Young Entrepreneur Program. We sent teams into two area high schools to help the students learn how to run their own businesses. Our executives taught them how to write a business plan, design an ad campaign, make sales calls, and deal with clients. We ended up hiring some of the kids as interns, which worked out really well.

The accomplishment this job candidate has chosen to highlight involves giving back to the community, which is certainly admirable. While it doesn't directly benefit the company in terms of sales or earnings, participation in a program like the one she describes is good for a company's public image.

Never Say: "My boss made me Senior Community Liaison. Finally having a title has been great." This candidate needs to focus on something she did in order to deserve that title.

 Question

What should I do if I'm a recent college graduate without many work-related accomplishments?
If you don't have much work experience, draw upon your experiences as a student. Look at what you achieved while you were in college, either in your classes or through extracurricular activities.

Q Do you consider your progress on your current job indicative of your ability?

A Yes, I do. I was promoted twice on my current job. I was hired as a marketing trainee. After about a year I was promoted to associate account executive, and then after two years I was promoted to account executive. My promotions came about because I proved that I could successfully meet deadlines, win the confidence of clients, and solve problems.

This candidate discusses how and why she was promoted.

Never Say: "Yes." This answer lacks specifics.

Q Describe how you accomplished a work-related goal.

A When I started working for Daylight Publications, I discovered that I had inherited a huge file cabinet full of photographs. We used photographs in our magazine but usually wound up purchasing stock photos, because our own collection was so disorganized it was impossible to find anything. I designed a filing system and set about putting things in order. I set aside fifteen minutes each day and was able to work my way through the whole collection in about seven months.

This answer demonstrates how the interviewee took the initiative to set a goal in order to save her employer money. She then talks about how she reached that goal by using her organization and time-management skills.

Never Say: "I wanted to make $50,000 per year by the time I was twenty-six. I switched jobs a few times and was able to do it." This in no way demonstrates any job-related skills the interviewee has.

Q Can you describe how you accomplished a personal goal?

A I wrote a short story, and my goal was to get it published. I went to the library and researched which magazines accepted short-story submissions. Then I sent my story to those publications that published stories in the same genre as mine. My story was accepted by one of them and was published a little over a year ago.

This candidate talks about the steps he took to reach his personal goal. While the goal isn't related to the job for which he is applying, he talks about his ability to do research, a skill he knows this prospective employer will value.

Never Say: "I won a hot dog–eating contest. I trained for about six months." This answer does not demonstrate any skills that are needed in the workplace.

Q Tell me how you were of value to your previous employer.

A My previous employer valued my ability to deal with difficult clients. Whenever we had a client who was very demanding, my boss would ask me to be the one to work with her. He said he knew I was so levelheaded that I would always stay calm, even when a client was really trying my patience.

By giving this answer, the candidate not only says why she thinks her boss values her, but she talks about it from her boss's perspective. She presents a skill that this employer will appreciate as well.

Never Say: "I always showed up on time." Showing up on time is expected and doesn't set this candidate apart from any other.

Q Have you ever had to take over an assignment at the last minute?

A I've had to do that more than once—actually several times. The most recent time was when a colleague was scheduled to attend a meeting out of town and came down with the flu two days before he was supposed to leave. My boss asked me if I could attend the meeting and make the presentation my colleague was supposed to make. I had two days to learn everything about the project. I went over pages and pages of notes and put together a presentation of my own, incorporating input from my colleague, whom I spoke to on the phone several times a day.

Not only does this interviewee say she has taken over an assignment at the last minute, she talks about a specific case. She shows how she stepped in and learned what she needed to learn in order to make a successful presentation.

Never Say: "Yes, it has happened." Give an example.

Q Have you ever received formal recognition for something you accomplished?

A Yes. I won Salesperson of the Month four times when I was working for Ace Stereo. Those with the largest increase in sales over the previous month were rewarded in this way. I believe I had increased my sales by 15 to 20 percent each time.

This candidate chose to discuss being rewarded for something that would be valued by any company—high sales volume. He gives actual numbers to quantify his answer.

Never Say: "I won Best Dressed at the annual holiday party." Unless this is a candidate for a fashion-consulting position, this answer doesn't highlight any skills that will impress the employer.

Q What has been your greatest accomplishment as part of a team?

A I worked on a team that developed a program for children who were going home to an empty house after school because their parents worked. We had volunteers who would help the kids with their homework and give them time to just burn off energy after sitting in a classroom all day. By the time we actually opened the center, we had seventy-five children enrolled. That told us we were providing a service that was clearly needed.

This candidate describes in detail the project she considers the greatest accomplishment she achieved as part of a team. She talks about what was needed, what they did to fill that need, and what the end result was.

Never Say: "I never feel like I accomplish that much on a team." This candidate just admitted she's not a team player. It was a bad idea to do that. The interviewer probably asked the question because working on a team is probably typical of the position for which he is hiring.

Q Name the two work-related accomplishments of which you are proudest.

A I converted a manual payroll system to a computerized system, which cuts down the amount of time we spend on payroll each week. I also wrote a manual that explained all bookkeeping department procedures in our company. New employees receive a copy of this manual, which helps them learn their job faster.

Each of the accomplishments this candidate discusses has had a positive result on the company and highlights his many skills.

Never Say: "I received a good performance review every year. I was promoted to a supervisory position after just two years." While these are definitely positive things and a reflection of this candidate's ability to do a good job, they really don't address how his accomplishments affected the company. They also don't explain how he earned his good reviews and promotion.

Q Tell me about the personal accomplishment that you are the proudest of.

A Last year I ran a marathon for the first time. I've been a runner for years, but I never ran more than four miles at a time. I began training four months before the big day. It was hard, but I kept going and ended up finishing in just over four hours, which I've heard is pretty good for a first-time marathoner.

By discussing running a marathon, this candidate demonstrates that she will work hard to reach her goals. She also shows that she is not afraid of a challenge, something her prospective employer should appreciate.

Never Say: "I bought my first house." Without an explanation of how she reached this goal, this candidate doesn't show off any strengths when she gives this example.

Q If I asked your current employer to tell us about your accomplishments, what do you think he would say?

A He would probably talk about the time he asked me to present a new marketing campaign to one of our more difficult clients.

I spent over a week preparing for that presentation. Since I knew this client was hard to please, I had to make sure I anticipated every objection she might have. She actually loved the presentation, and the campaign increased her company's sales by 50 percent.

This question gives the candidate a chance to talk about an accomplishment he is proud of. He talks about anticipating possible difficulties as well as the end result, an increase in sales.

Never Say: "I doubt my boss recognized any of my accomplishments. If he did, he certainly didn't tell me." This candidate breaks one of the cardinal rules of job interviewing—to never speak negatively about a former boss.

Q Have you ever had to overcome a major obstacle? How did you do it?

A Yes, I did. My family couldn't afford to pay for college. I applied for as much financial aid as possible, but I still had to work to pay for whatever that didn't cover. I worked after classes every day and on the weekends, too. In the end, in addition to a college degree, I also had some valuable work experience under my belt.

The story this candidate tells demonstrates that she can set a goal—getting a college degree—and reach it through hard work. She even points out that, because of her need to overcome this obstacle, she now has valuable work experience.

Never Say: "I've been very lucky. I really haven't had any obstacles to overcome." Luck isn't what is going to get this candidate hired. She needs to demonstrate perseverance and therefore should try to find some obstacle to speak about.

Q What motivates you to go above and beyond the call of duty?

A Honestly, I don't have a sense of what is above and beyond the call of duty. It's not like I can just do enough to get by and then stop. When I work on a project, I do my very best, always.

This statement shows that this job candidate is truly a hard worker who cares about her work. It's more than just a job to her. She can't justify giving less than her best effort to any project entrusted to her.

Never Say: "Hopefully, if I go above and beyond the call of duty, I'll get recognition for my work." This candidate doesn't seem to be self-motivated, since her rewards come from the outside.

Q What one thing do you think you've done very well on your last job?

A I think I was very successful in all aspects of my last job. I'm particularly proud of my work with new hires. I developed programs that helped integrate them into the company and this in turn helped our ability to retain them as employees.

Because the interviewer has asked for one thing this person has done well, he is forced to only talk about one thing. He explains why he is particularly proud of that one accomplishment and explains how his success benefited his employer. He also makes a point of saying that this isn't his only success.

Never Say: "I can't think of just one thing." If you are asked for one thing, you should be able to come up with something. If not, it appears that you can't think of anything you did well at your last job.

Q You seem to have accomplished a lot in your current job. Do you know why you weren't promoted?

A I wasn't promoted because unfortunately there wasn't a position to promote me to. JFR was a very small, family-owned firm. The boss's two sons held the top positions, which were right above my position.

The candidate explains why he couldn't move beyond his current position in spite of his accomplishments. He doesn't seem resentful, but rather accepts this fact.

Never Say: "Sure I do. One word—nepotism. The boss's sons hold all the good positions. It doesn't matter how hard you work. You aren't moving up." This candidate is clearly resentful of the way things are at his current job and makes the mistake of letting the interviewer know that.

Q Have you ever come up with new ways to solve a problem?

A Yes, I have. We had a problem with dismissal from our after-school program. Too many children were leaving at once, causing chaos in our parking lot. I developed a system for releasing children alphabetically so that parents could pick up siblings in different grades at the same time. If we had released children by grade, parents would have had to wait around for children who were in different grade levels. That would have added to the chaos.

The candidate states a specific problem and then discusses the steps she took to solve it. She even mentions how she anticipated and then prevented a potential problem.

Never Say: "I'm lucky. I haven't had to solve any problems." If this candidate hasn't had to solve any problems, how can she be expected to do so in the future?

Q Have you ever been asked to take on a project because of your unique skill or ability?

A Our senior developer regularly asks me to troubleshoot new programs. I've been very successful at figuring out why programs aren't working properly, and I can usually do it pretty quickly, allowing the team to move forward.

This candidate chose to talk about a skill that will be as valuable to his prospective employer as it is to his current one.

Never Say: "I'm very good at planning parties, so when my boss's secretary was retiring, she asked me to plan the party." This skill probably won't be very important to the prospective employer.

Q Have you ever done something that directly helped your employer either increase profits or decrease costs?

A I recently found a way to help my employer save money on office supplies. For years, they bought office supplies from the same place. It was several blocks away, so it was pretty convenient. I have found that shopping online is almost always less expensive than shopping in a store, so I did a little comparison shopping and I found an online source for our office supplies at a savings of 40 percent from what we were paying for the same items. Plus, the order is delivered to the office, which is even more convenient. As long as we order several items at once, delivery is free.

This interviewee's answer illustrates how he looks out for his employer's best interests.

Never Say: "I just go about doing my job. I guess that increases their profits, doesn't it?" This candidate needs to remember he's trying to sell himself to this employer. Instead of saying he'll "just do the job," he needs to show why he'd be great at it.

Q It seems like you've accomplished a lot. I know everyone fails, at least occasionally. Tell me about something you failed at.

A When I was a freshman in college, I decided to run for president of the management club. My opponent was in his junior year. I came up with what I thought and still think was a great platform. I campaigned vigorously. Unfortunately, I lost the election. I'm pretty sure it was due to my lack of experience. I ran too early in my school career. Two years later I ran again and I won.

The applicant chooses to discuss a failure that isn't work-related and attributes it to her lack of experience rather than something she had control over.

Never Say: "I ran for president of the management club and lost." The applicant must give a more detailed answer. This one leaves the interviewer to wonder why the applicant lost the election.

Q Is there anything I've missed?

A Well, I did want to mention that I was honored by my organization's board of directors for developing a program that reached out to a large number of senior citizens in need of financial assistance. We now help just over 650 seniors each year.

The candidate uses this opportunity to bring to the interviewer's attention an accomplishment he didn't discuss previously.

Never Say: "No. I think you just about covered it all. Are we done?" This candidate sounds like he's in a hurry for the interview to be over. Since it is unlikely that everything has been covered, he may be missing a chance to discuss something that can work in his favor.

CHAPTER 8

Questions about Your Education

When prospective employers interview recent graduates without much experience, they can learn a lot about them by asking questions about their school experience. Therefore, if you're interviewing for jobs straight out of school, you should be prepared to answer a lot of questions about your education. Even if you've been working for a few years, you may still be asked about your education, so it's important to have your answers ready.

How You Spent Your College Years

The interviewer will want to know about your performance as a student. As you know, the grades on a college transcript don't always tell the whole story. A failing grade may mean more than an inability in a particular subject, and a high grade may mean more than great achievement.

The interviewer will want to know how you felt about particular subjects, which ones you found challenging, and which ones you thought were a piece of cake. She may ask which instructors you liked and why. All of this information lets her get a better look at who you are.

In addition to simple questions like "Where did you go to school?" and "What was your major?" the interviewer will likely ask you about activities you participated in outside the classroom. She will want to know about your involvement in extracurricular activities, such as participation in on-campus clubs and organizations, work on student-run publications, and community service. All these activities contributed to your education and make up who you are today—and what you will bring to an employer. Think about your activities in terms of the skills they helped you develop. When you can't prove your worth by talking about your work experience, you must prove it by discussing what you did during your time in school.

 Essential

When asked about extracurricular activities, you should think of each one as a job. What contributions did you make to a particular club? Can you quantify them? Did you help raise money for a charity? How much? Did you work for your school newspaper? How many hours a week did that involve? What were your successes and what were your failures?

Many students gain valuable work experience by doing an internship. If you did one, be prepared to discuss it in great detail. Even if you didn't get paid, you should consider it equivalent to a job. The interviewer will want to know what you did there, what you learned, and what contributions you made.

The prospective employer has something else on her agenda too. She is interested in knowing why and how you made your choices over the last several years. For example, she wants to know how you chose what college to attend. She wants to find out how you decided on your major. Seeing how you made these very important choices gives her the opportunity to learn what your decision-making process is generally like.

Questions and Answers

Q I see you majored in English. Are you prepared for a job in marketing and sales?

A As an English major, I had to do a large amount of reading and needed to retain all of the information. Reading and absorbing the literature on the products I'll be selling will be a snap. I believe college also prepared me to manage my time well. I do have hands-on experience in this field as well; I worked in various sales positions in order to put myself through school.

Notice that the interviewee doesn't make any excuses for wanting to work in a field outside his major. Instead, he talks about how his major qualifies him for this job. He also talks about the fact that he has sales experience.

Never Say: "I guess I could teach at a college with my English degree, but then I'd have to get a PhD. I definitely don't want to do that." The interviewer knows what this applicant doesn't want to do, but she still doesn't know how the interviewee can transfer his skills to this field.

Q Why did you choose Adams University?

A Adams University has an accredited business school. It's ranked third in the nation. The university also has a great cross-country team, and I wanted to try out for it.

This candidate put a lot of thought into choosing a college, implying that's how she makes all her decisions. She also uses this opportunity to brag about the quality of her education.

Never Say: "My best friend was going there." This applicant doesn't demonstrate that she puts a lot of thought into making important decisions.

Q Did you have any teachers who influenced you?

A Yes, I did. It goes all the way back to junior high school. Mr. Danzer was my earth science teacher. He loved the subject and he loved teaching. I think both these things came across in his ability to teach. It showed me that if a person loves what he does, he's more likely to excel at it. That was good to know when it came time to choose a career.

This candidate answers the question with just enough information to satisfy the interviewer.

Never Say: "No." If you can't think of one single teacher, perhaps you can mention the qualities of several who had some sort of impact on you.

 Question

> **What should I do if my major and my career choice are unrelated?** If you did not major in a subject that traditionally prepares people to work in the career field you are pursuing, you are going to have some explaining to do. Be ready to discuss how your major prepared you for this occupation even though they are seemingly unrelated to one another.

Q Why did you choose to major in philosophy?

A From a very early age I wanted to be a lawyer. When I started to do my research, I found out that undergraduates who want to go to law school should take a lot of liberal arts classes. During my freshman year, I took different courses in the school of liberal arts and sciences and I liked philosophy the best, so I decided to make it my concentration.

This applicant shows that she made an informed choice when choosing her major.

Never Say: "It looked interesting." While you should choose a major you think is interesting, that shouldn't be your only criteria.

Q What did you gain from attending college?

A I gained knowledge about this field. I was able to use what I learned in class on the internship I did last summer at the *Tallahassee Tribune*. College is where I learned to be independent. There wasn't anyone pushing me to complete assignments on time, so I had to learn how to manage my time well and stay organized.

This candidate talks about things he learned both in and out of the classroom. He includes technical skills as well as soft skills— time management and organization.

Never Say: "I got my degree." Isn't that on the resume? The candidate needs to come up with a more detailed answer than this one.

Q What was your favorite subject in high school? What was your favorite subject in college?

A English was my favorite subject in high school. I did a lot of writing in English. I liked working hard to put together a paper and then getting feedback in the form of a grade. My favorite classes in college were those in my major. I actually took only one marketing class before I declared marketing as my major. I found the subject matter so interesting that I started looking into it as a career choice.

This candidate explains why English was her favorite subject and in the process demonstrates her skill as a writer, which she knows will be an important part of her job. By stating that her major was her favorite subject in college, she shows her dedication to the field.

Never Say: "In high school I liked social studies. My favorite subject in college was sociology." This candidate needs to explain why these two subjects were her favorites.

Q What were your least favorite subjects in high school and college?

●A My least favorite subject in high school was home economics. I helped with the housekeeping at home, and I didn't want to have to deal with it at school, too. I liked most of the classes I took in college. If I had to pick my least favorite, I guess it would have to be biology. We had to dissect a fetal pig, and I had a problem doing that.

The candidate picked classes unrelated to the job for which he's applying. Also notice that he didn't say he disliked the classes because he found them difficult. Never imply that you don't like challenges.

Never Say: "My least favorite classes were geometry and matrix algebra. I couldn't get it. I guess math isn't my strong suit." This candidate makes the mistake of volunteering information about his weaknesses. While they may not be related to this job, they are challenges that defeated him.

 Alert

If the interviewer asks what your least favorite class was, pick one that is as unrelated as possible to your career field. If your least favorite class is one in which you received a failing grade, pick another one. Don't bring up a failing grade unless you are asked a direct question about it.

Q What extracurricular activities did you participate in?

A During my junior year of college, I was president of the psychology club. Then in my senior year, I was editor of the yearbook. I wrote for both my high school and college newspapers too.

This candidate highlights her leadership experience and writing skills, two very valuable attributes.

Never Say: "Academics took up all my time. I didn't have much time for anything else." This candidate may think she's showing what a dedicated student she was, but extracurricular activities enhance one's college experience. She should try to think of some valuable experience she had outside the classroom.

Q I see it took you four and a half years to graduate. Can you explain that?

A I had a difficult time adjusting during my freshman year. I wasn't quite ready for all the demands of college. I had to take a few classes over. During the summer between my freshman and sophomore years, I went to a few workshops to help me improve my study skills and my time management skills. By the time I was a sophomore, I was a much more serious student.

This candidate doesn't make excuses for his failings, but rather speaks about how he overcame them and how he succeeded in the end.

Never Say: "I had these really tough professors my freshman year. They wouldn't cut me any slack. When you're a freshman, you get stuck with teachers no one else wants." This candidate tries to blame everyone else for his failure.

Q Aside from coursework, what was the most enriching part of your college education?

A I was very involved on the programming committee. As a matter of fact, I was chair during my senior year. We were responsible for planning on-campus events for the student body. The goal was to hold events that were well attended and safe. That meant hiring entertainment that appealed to the majority of students and making sure campus security was present to enforce the rules. Our events were attended by between 60 and 70 percent of dormitory residents.

This applicant talks about her work on this committee as if it were a job. She highlights her leadership skills as well as other skills she drew upon in order to organize these events. This candidate also explains her goals and how she met them, giving actual numbers.

Never Say: "I was in some campus clubs and that was fun." This applicant needs to do a better job of explaining what those clubs were and how she participated in them.

Q I see you had an internship in this field. What did you learn from it?

A My internship at Carlson Corporate allowed me to get some hands-on experience in this field that I wouldn't have gotten in classes alone. I learned that jobs in this field are often stressful, and long hours are usually required. On the other hand, I got to find out how wonderful it is when you're on a team that helps land a big account as a result of hard work.

This applicant speaks about what he gained from the internship and what he learned about the positive and negative aspects of working in the field.

Never Say: "Not a heck of a lot. I was just a glorified gopher." Even if all he did was deliver mail and make copies, this candidate should be able to come up with something he learned just from being exposed to the work environment of this particular field.

Q Why haven't you done any internships?

A I would have loved to have done an internship, but unfortunately I had to work my way through college. Most internships don't pay that well. However, as you can see from my resume, I made a point of finding work within this industry. Even though I was in the mailroom, I was still exposed to the field.

While internships are important, sometimes extenuating circumstances get in the way. This candidate has no choice but to be honest about that. However, she explains how she tried to make up for not being able to do an internship.

Never Say: "I won't work for free." This candidate sounds like she's only concerned with money and experience is worth nothing to her.

Q How did you spend your summers during college?

A I worked every summer to earn money for books and part of my tuition. I had this great job at a day camp. I started off as a counselor the summer before my senior year of high school, moved up to group leader the summer after I graduated, and then became assistant director.

This applicant takes the opportunity to show off a little. He stayed at the same job for several years and was promoted to a supervisory position.

Never Say: "I rested. School's hard." If he thinks school is hard, wait until he tries working—he probably won't get two months off each year.

Q What grade did you receive in your favorite class?

A My favorite class was Intro to Journalism. It was actually pretty tough at first. Everything I handed in came back marked up in red ink. I must have gotten Ds on the first four assignments. There were a few times that my professor commented that I had found just the right words to describe an event, though, and I loved that feeling. I plugged away and kept trying harder. Fortunately, my professor gave us the opportunity to redo our work for a higher grade, and although it took a lot of extra work, ultimately I got an A in the class.

It's easy to like a class if you don't have to work hard for a good grade. This applicant explains why journalism was her favorite class despite it being difficult. Perseverance and the ability to meet a challenge are attributes all bosses value in their employees.

Never Say: "Intro to Journalism. I got an A." Without saying more than that, the interviewer is left to wonder whether the candidate liked that class simply because she got an A in it.

Q What grade did you receive in your least favorite class?

A My least favorite class was Art History. I know students who took the class with other professors, got a C, and loved it. I hated the class and got an A. I didn't learn anything. I just had to show up for every class and do little else.

Clearly this candidate doesn't mind working hard as long as he learns something. He isn't impressed with getting rewarded for "just showing up."

Never Say: "I got a D in it. It was Organic Chemistry, the hardest class I ever took. I can't believe how much I studied and all I ended up with was a D." Other than getting a bad grade, this candidate doesn't explain why this was his least favorite class. He just sounds like a sore loser.

 Essential

How you spend your summers while in school says a lot. Your experience may not be career related, but provides the opportunity to highlight positive qualities about yourself. Were you asked back to the same job summer after summer? Your prospective employer can assume that is because of good job performance.

Q Why did you decide to major in elementary education?

A When I was in high school, I took an assessment test to help me figure out what career I should go into. When I got my results, teaching was one of the occupations on the list, along with several others like psychology, social work, and nursing. When I started researching the occupations in more detail, I discovered that teaching was the one that appealed to me most.

This candidate put a lot of thought into choosing an occupation. This answer not only shows her dedication to teaching but also indicates that she makes decisions carefully.

Never Say: "I like children." While it's important to like children if you want to teach them, liking children doesn't necessarily mean you'll be good at teaching.

Q What courses best prepared you for a job in this library?

A I took a course in research and bibliographic methods that provided me with the technical skills to do this job. The most important thing I learned in that class was that there is a resource available to answer almost all questions. I also took several classes in children's and young adult literature. I saw from the job description that the person who takes this position will also have to spend several hours a week in the children's department. Those courses have certainly helped prepare me for that.

This candidate not only lists some courses he took, but also explains how they will help him do the job should he be hired.

Never Say: "I took research and bibliographic methods and some children's lit classes. I think they'll be helpful." This candidate tells what classes he took but isn't specific about how they will enable him to do his job.

Q Are you planning to get your MBA?

A I would like to do that. I'm looking for a program with a schedule that won't interfere with work.

This interviewee knows that an MBA is highly valued in her field, but she anticipates that her potential employer might be concerned that her work schedule would be compromised if she pursues one. She heads off those fears.

Never Say: "I've already been accepted at NJU. The classes start at 5:45, so I'm hoping it will be okay if I cut out of here early three days a week." If the employer had a choice between this candidate and one who wouldn't need her schedule adjusted, whom do you think he would choose? In addition, any discussion of that sort should wait until a job offer is received.

Q What elective accounting courses did you take?

A I took three auditing classes because I knew I wanted to work in public accounting. I also took an international accounting class. In this global economy, I knew that would come in handy at some point in my career.

This candidate explains how she chose courses she would be able to use professionally.

Never Say: "I took a taxation class, an auditing class, and a corporate accounting class that all fit nicely into my schedule." This answer doesn't show that the candidate selected classes that would benefit her in her career.

Q Have you ever had a disagreement with a professor? How did you handle it?

A I disagreed about a grade I received once. I spent a lot of time researching and writing a paper for a history class. When I got the paper back with a B, I was very disappointed. After thinking about it for a day, I decided to talk to the professor. He asked me what grade I thought I deserved. I said I thought I had earned an A on the paper and explained why. He said he would read the paper over and re-grade it if he found my arguments were valid. The next day he told me he changed my grade to an A.

This applicant proves that she knows how to stand up for herself when there is something she feels strongly about. She demonstrates how she persuaded her teacher to change her grade by presenting her arguments in a calm manner after waiting a day to collect her thoughts.

Never Say: "I was very unhappy about a grade a professor gave me, but I didn't bother saying anything about it."

Q What was the most difficult assignment you had while in school?

A I took a creative writing class. It was one of several electives I could choose from outside my major. I had to write a poem. I discovered I'm not really good at that sort of thing.

This interviewee chose to discuss an assignment that was entirely unrelated to his major and to anything he would be expected to do at this job.

Never Say: "I hated writing papers, so any assignment that involved doing that was difficult." Since some writing is generally required at all jobs, this candidate should have answered differently.

Q What did you like most about college?

A I really enjoyed playing on the volleyball team. During my freshman and sophomore years, the team wasn't as strong as it could have been. We pulled together and worked very hard, and by my junior year we were ranked number two in our division. By my senior year we were in first place.

This candidate's mention of his participation on an athletic team draws attention to his ability to work on a team. From his research, he learned that this company's employees often work on teams, so he decided this was a good opportunity to show off this attribute.

Never Say: "I loved my classes." While that is admirable, this candidate doesn't say why this is so. If his classes were truly his favorite part of college, he needs to explain how his own actions contributed to his feeling that way.

Q Why didn't you go to college?

A I didn't know what I wanted to do at the time, and I didn't want to waste my parents' money. I thought I would gain more from working than I would from school. Now that I have work experience and know I want to stay in this field, I plan to get my degree. The city university has a program that accommodates working adults.

The interviewee's decision to postpone college, as he explains it, was a clearly thought-out one. While he indicates his intention to continue his education, he is also quick to point out that it won't affect his work schedule.

Never Say: "I don't know. I didn't really give it much thought." Not giving a lot of thought to such an important decision doesn't say much about this applicant, or maybe it says too much.

Q Why didn't you finish college?

A I left school because of financial reasons. My parents couldn't afford my tuition, so I decided to work for a few years. The experience was actually a great one for me. I learned a lot from it. I'm planning to take some classes next semester. I just heard about a great program that offers classes online. I even checked the program out with the state education department and it's legitimate.

Dropping out of school for financial reasons is certainly legitimate. This candidate speaks positively of her work experience, claiming she gained something from it. She goes on to explain how her plan to take some classes won't affect her work schedule, something the employer would probably appreciate.

Never Say: "I didn't really like school that much." This interviewee gives the impression that she doesn't make well-informed decisions.

CHAPTER 9

Discussing Your Work History

While experience isn't everything, it does count for a lot when a prospective employer must decide between you and other qualified candidates. What you have done in your past jobs is significant, and an interviewer will spend a lot of time learning about your work history so he can discover how it will affect your future performance. That is why it is so important that you take great care to present your past well.

How to Present Your Past

What does it mean to present your past well? After years of spending many of your waking hours working, here's a chance to let past jobs work for you. Answering questions about your work history gives you the opportunity to highlight things you want to call to a prospective employer's attention. At the same time, you want to downplay things on which you would rather not have her focus. You want to tell your side of the story in your own words and in greater depth than you could ever do on a resume.

When prospective employers ask questions about your work history, they want to know more than where you worked, how long you worked there, and what your job duties were. They can learn that from your resume. They would love to hear about the skills you gained at each of your previous jobs, but that information is probably on your resume as well. Now it's time to get beyond the resume and learn more about you than they ever could from a one- or two-page document. Employers want to know not only what skills you picked up on your prior jobs, but how you used those skills. They want to know what you liked about each job and what you didn't like. They want to find out if you got along with your boss. Employers want to know why you left each of your jobs, or why you stayed. They want to know what motivates you. They want to know how your career has progressed and how you expect it to in the future. Most importantly, employers want to know what you can bring to them.

 Essential

As you prepare to answer questions about your work history, use your resume to guide you. Look at each job and try to recall specific details about every one. Write down those facts and commit them to memory. Preparing in advance can help save you from awkward moments of silence as you try to answer a prospective employer's questions.

When you give answers to questions about your work history, make every one count. Each response should tell the interviewer how your experience qualifies you for this particular job. You should give specific examples drawn from your experiences. When an interviewer asks if you've ever performed a particular activity on a past job, she generally expects more than a yes or no answer. As with every type of question so far, you must give detailed answers.

Questions and Answers

Q Out of the jobs you've had, which was your favorite?

A My favorite job was teaching at the Wee Ones Preschool. I like my current job at Parkside Elementary, but I realize now that I prefer to work with preschoolers. That's why I want to work here.

This candidate has chosen to discuss a job that is related to the one for which she is being interviewed.

Never Say: "I loved working at Sam's Steakhouse in college. The other waitresses and I had so much fun together." Not only does this candidate choose a job unrelated to her chosen field, she doesn't sound very serious about working at all.

Q Tell me about your current job.

A I am a junior architect at James, Jones, and Johnson. I work in the commercial building division. As part of a team of five architects, I help design shopping centers and office complexes.

The interviewee describes his current job as he is asked to do. He discusses his work as part of a team because he knows that this prospective employer also utilizes a team structure.

Never Say: "I work at James, Jones, and Johnson. It's right there on my resume." The interviewer wants the candidate to give a detailed description of his current job. Since it is probable that he has already read the resume, it does the candidate no good to simply reiterate what is there.

Q Tell me about a typical day at work.

A Every day is different. The one constant is that I spend from two to three hours working at the reference desk each day, assisting patrons. That leaves either four or five hours to tend to what I refer to as "behind the scenes" work. I'm in charge of library publicity, so I might have to write and send out press releases or update our mailing list. If it's the middle of the month, I'll be working on the monthly newsletter. When I'm not working on publicity, I'm selecting books to order or weeding outdated material from our collection.

The candidate takes this opportunity to discuss her many responsibilities.

Never Say: "Every day is different. I do so many things, it's hard to say what a typical day is." This person indicates she's busy, but she needs to talk about what her responsibilities are.

Q What do you like about your job?

A I like it when I can successfully resolve a customer's problem. If the customer walks away satisfied, I'm happy.

By giving this answer, the candidate shows that keeping customers happy motivates him. This is surely something this employer will see as a positive trait, since happy customers are repeat customers.

Never Say: "My boss is nice." While speaking well of your boss is good, this candidate should have chosen something about his job that gives him satisfaction.

Essential

> When you are asked to discuss something you like about your job, choose something that is related to your work. Talk about job duties, specifically ones that are related to those you will have if the company with which you are interviewing hires you. Try to demonstrate how you have benefited your employer by performing these tasks well.

Q Describe your favorite boss.

A That would have to be my boss at Triangle Optical. Paul was the most demanding boss I've ever had. He expected so much from our department. What set him apart from other supervisors was that he worked tirelessly alongside us and was just as demanding of himself. He always gave everyone the credit they deserved.

This applicant values having a demanding boss. In addition, by telling her prospective employer what traits she valued in a former boss, this applicant is letting him know what she will be like as a supervisor if she is hired for this job.

Never Say: "I like a boss who is flexible and fair." While the candidate doesn't reveal anything negative by giving this answer, she should be more specific.

Q Describe your least favorite boss.

A I'd rather not mention names, since this industry is so small. I had a boss who never planned anything in advance. We were always racing to meet deadlines, running out of supplies, or finding ourselves short staffed because she couldn't say no to anyone who asked for a day off.

While it's generally best not to say something negative about a former employer, the interviewee must answer the question. In saying he won't reveal the name of his least favorite boss, he demonstrates tact and discretion. He is also somewhat restrained in his criticism. All this candidate says is that he prefers someone who is more structured. Rejecting his former boss's management style implies that this is not what he'd be like as a manager.

Never Say: "Her name was Josephine Josephson, and she was my boss at BRK Audio. She was too demanding." This applicant doesn't hesitate to reveal his boss's name and doesn't give enough of a reason for choosing her as his worst boss. The interviewer may be left wondering why he considered this person too demanding.

Q You seem to be climbing the corporate ladder in your current job. Why leave now?

A I'm choosing to leave now because my goals have changed. I feel I can better use my public relations skills at a nonprofit organization such as this one.

This applicant is making a change to another industry, but shows how she can still utilize her skills to meet her new goals.

Never Say: "My bosses are crazy. I can't stay there anymore." Remember that making negative comments about any employer is a bad idea.

Q I see three jobs listed on your resume. Can you tell me what you learned from each of them?

A I learned a lot on each of my jobs, so it's hard to pick one thing from each, but I'll try. When I worked in customer support at CSV, I learned how to help our software users troubleshoot problems. When I worked as a software trainer at Circle Tech, I learned that I needed to find a common ground when teaching a large group of people, because not everyone has the same level of skills. I learned to manage employees at my job as assistant to the head of training at APCO.

Knowing about the job that he's applying for helped the applicant answer this question. He has picked one skill from each of his previous jobs that will be required for the position with this employer.

Never Say: "I learned to be at work on time from my first job. Then from my second job, I learned to keep my mouth shut." While it's good that the applicant has learned these things, they don't demonstrate why he will be a valuable employee.

Q Do you find your job rewarding?

A I found my job very rewarding for a long time, but lately it hasn't been as rewarding. While I love my new responsibilities, I miss working with clients. That is what attracted me to this position—the combination of supervisory responsibilities and client contact.

It's okay for the interviewee to say she doesn't find her current job rewarding. She explains why she feels this way without placing blame anywhere. With this answer, she also shows she knows about the position for which she's interviewing and explains why she is better suited for it.

Never Say: "No, I don't. When the new manager came in, he took away everything I liked about my job." This candidate sounds angry.

Q What about your current job isn't very rewarding?

A I think every job has something about it that isn't rewarding. There is a lot of paperwork and I don't find that particularly rewarding, but I know it needs to be done.

This candidate understands the reality of work. Some job duties are rewarding, while others are not. She chose something that many people don't find particularly rewarding—paperwork.

Never Say: "Everything about it is rewarding." The interviewer, who knows every job has things about it that are not rewarding, will question this applicant's sincerity. Furthermore, he will wonder why the applicant is leaving her current job if she finds everything about it rewarding.

Q How have your other jobs prepared you for the one at this company?

A I've worked on the retail end of the office supplies industry for the past ten years. I know what customers want and what the retail outlets want. I know the industry and I know the products. That is what qualifies me to be a sales rep for Roxy Staple Company.

This candidate shows confidence in her abilities as a salesperson and in her knowledge of the industry of which the prospective employer is a part.

Never Say: "I learned a lot on my previous jobs. My skills qualify me for a job with your company." By giving such a brief answer, the interviewer will have to follow up with the question, "Which skills would those be?"

Q Your last job was very different than the ones you had before it and very different than this one. Why did you take that job?

A I was thinking of going back to school to be a veterinarian. I mentioned this to my neighbor, a vet, and he offered me a job in his office. I love animals, but before I made the commitment to go to veterinary school, I wanted to make sure I'd be happy working with them and especially dealing with sick ones. It turned out that wasn't right for me after all.

This candidate has a good explanation for why she took a job that deviated from her career path. In providing it, she also shows off her decision-making skills—she didn't jump into a new career without careful consideration.

Never Say: "The job was available and they wanted to hire me." This candidate had no particular reason for taking a job outside her field, leading the potential employer to question her goals.

Q You've never worked in widget manufacturing before. How have your jobs in the publishing industry prepared you for this?

A Taking a product, whether it's a widget or a book, from its inception to the hands of the consumer takes a lot of planning. You have to put together a budget and set deadlines. You need to make sure your current staff can handle the work and hire consultants if necessary. You may even have to handle crises along the way, should problems arise. I dealt with such things on a daily basis while working in publishing, and I would be able to use the same planning and management skills to help your company.

By focusing on her job responsibilities and talking about them in general terms, this candidate is able to show how she can transfer her skills from one industry to another.

Never Say: "I had to work long hours in publishing, and I know people in your industry work long hours, too." This doesn't tell the interviewer much about the candidate or what skills she has.

 Essential

When discussing what you would do if you were hired, you should draw on your past experience. Talk about how you completed similar projects on your last job or how you made similar decisions.

Q How would your current supervisor describe you?

A Mr. Roberts respects me. He would describe me as a diligent worker who takes great care to do an excellent job on every project he assigns to me. I complete all work on time. He appreciates the fact that I am very friendly and usually asks me to be our department's "welcome wagon" when a new employee starts.

A little bit of bragging on a job interview is a good thing. This applicant knows that to answer with anything less than this amount of confidence might lead the interviewer to think she's unsure of herself.

Never Say: "I've worked there for three years and he's never complained." Saying your boss never complained about you doesn't exactly shout "great employee!"

Q What decisions have you had to make on your current job?

A When I planned career workshops for students, I had to decide what topics to feature, when to hold the workshops, and who would speak at them. I had to decide what software to purchase for our public computers within the constraints of our budget. I also made decisions about hiring and firing student aides.

By giving specific examples, this candidate highlights his skills in planning events, making purchasing decisions, working within a budget, and making personnel decisions.

Never Say: "I didn't really get to make too many decisions." This applicant should realize the interviewer is asking this question because decision making is required on this job. He should take a moment to think of one or two decisions he has made. Even if they don't seem significant, it is better than not giving an answer.

Q What were the reasons you went to work for your two prior employers?

A I went to work for Pear Computers right out of college. They had an excellent one-year training program, and I knew I would learn a lot there. After I completed the training program, I stayed there for three years. I went to work for my next employer, Bell Technology, because they offered me a position with greater responsibilities than Pear Computers could.

This candidate takes advantage of the opportunity to mention her participation in a training program where she was able to enhance what she learned in school. When she says she stayed at the company for a while after taking part in the training program, she demonstrates her loyalty—she didn't just take the training and run. Her next job was clearly a step up from her first one, which shows how her career has progressed so far.

Never Say: "Each of my last two employers offered a good salary and benefits." This applicant should better demonstrate how she makes decisions. More thought should go into choosing to work for someone.

Q Why did you leave your last job?

A I left my last job because I knew the industry was facing an uncertain future. I researched this industry, saw the growth potential, and knew I could make a significant contribution.

This job candidate shows that he knows how to plan for the future. He doesn't make decisions without doing his homework first.

Never Say: "I was bored." Without giving further explanation, this isn't a good enough reason to leave your job.

Q You've been at your job for several years. What makes you want to leave?

A I've completed what I set out to do. When I first started working there, the company was just getting started. They needed someone who had the skills to help them grow. They are very successful now, and I feel like I've completed my mission. I know I could better use my skills in a growing company such as yours.

Not only does this applicant show off her accomplishments at her current job, she tells her potential employer what she can do for his company.

Never Say: "I want to make more money." This may really be this candidate's reason for leaving her job, but it isn't a good enough one to give to a prospective employer.

Q What duties of your last job did you find difficult?

A I found it difficult to fire people. Even though I always put a lot of thought into deciding whether or not to terminate someone, I knew I was affecting someone's livelihood.

No one could fault someone for disliking this unpleasant duty.

Never Say: "Dealing with my boss every day." Oops.

Q Describe how your career progressed over the last five years. Was it aligned with the goals you set for yourself?

A When I graduated from the community college, I knew I wanted to be a store manager. I also knew I would have to work my way up, so I took a job as a sales associate at Dress Corral. After two years and a lot of hard work, I was promoted to assistant department manager. After being in that job for a year, P.J. Coopers hired me to be manager of the ladies' accessories department. I've been there for the last two years. With my experience, I'm ready for the next step—store manager.

This job candidate shows exactly how his career has progressed and how he is now ready for a job with this employer.

Never Say: "I really didn't set any goals. I took the sales associate job because it was the only place that wanted someone with my skills. It's been nice to be able to move up." It's okay if this candidate didn't have a plan to start with, but he should have made one along the way. It seems he's let others set goals for him. If he doesn't have a plan, this prospective employer can't predict what he'll do next.

 Alert

You should always make a point of sounding confident when answering questions on a job interview. If you sound unsure of yourself, the interviewer will pick up on it. Your confidence—or lack thereof—is also apparent in your body language, so be aware of what your posture and gestures say about you.

Q How would those who worked under you describe you as a supervisor?

A My staff at AQA Associates knew I was someone who worked hard and expected the same of them. They also felt I was fair, never asking them to do something I wasn't willing to do myself. My office door was always open, and they knew they could come to me to discuss any problem they might have.

This applicant describes the qualities of a good supervisor. Not only did she know exactly how she was regarded by staff, she tells him why they felt that way.

Never Say: "I think they thought I did a good job." The applicant doesn't provide enough information.

Q This job carries with it much more responsibility than you've had before. Are you ready?

A I am definitely ready. I've been working as assistant registrar for five years. I have learned a lot at Burberry College. I've worked very closely with my boss and I know what his job entails. He is also confident in my ability to move on.

This candidate restates her experience and shares with the interviewer the vote of confidence her boss gave her.

Never Say: "Sure. Why not? I've paid my dues."

Q Have you had to do any traveling for work?

A I've had to do some traveling for my job. I went to Asia several times. I enjoy traveling and hope to do more of it on this job. I find it helpful to have face-to-face meetings with clients periodically rather than doing everything through conference calls.

This applicant knows that his potential employer requires extensive traveling. Although he hasn't done a lot of it, he makes sure to point out that it's something he wants to do more.

Never Say: "They had me traveling all over the place." This candidate doesn't sound very enthusiastic.

Q What do you think this job offers that your last job did not?

A This job offers me the opportunity to use my research skills. I have mostly administrative duties at my current job, with some research duties. I look forward to a job that is primarily research oriented with some administrative duties.

This applicant has both administrative and research skills, as she points out to the interviewer. She wants to use them in a different way than she does on her current job. She knows, based on what she has learned about this position, that research is a big part of the job.

Never Say: "This job offers me the opportunity to do research. I've always wanted to do that." There's nothing to indicate that this person has any research skills. If there are many candidates to choose from, the employer may not be willing to hire someone who still requires training.

Q What was your salary when you started your current job and what is it now?

A I earned $40,000 per year when I started and now, after five years, I'm up to $50,000.

As long as this information is accurate, this is a good answer.

Never Say: "I'm not sure what I made when I started, but I'm making $50,000 per year now." The candidate should be ready to provide this information; if she truly doesn't know the answer, she can offer to provide it later.

CHAPTER 10

Your Interpersonal Skills

Wouldn't it be nice if everyone got along with one another? Unfortunately, a world in which everyone gets along is only a dream. There will always be personality conflicts and differences of opinion, whether they are within families, on the playground, or at work. What is important is how we deal with them when they occur. If handled well, they can lead to new ideas and growth.

An Employee Balancing Act

Each time an employer introduces a new member to his company or department, he disturbs a delicate balance. Depending on how well the new employee gets along with her new coworkers, this addition may completely tip the scales in one direction or another, or they may move only slightly.

Employers ask personal questions so they can learn about your personality or character traits. One reason they want to know about this is so they can determine whether you will fit in with the other employees. These character traits are only a piece of the puzzle, however. A potential employee may have skills and experience that make her the most qualified candidate, but her character traits may differ greatly from those of other employees. This probably won't matter to the employer as long as the candidate knows how to make the most of those differences instead of getting sidetracked by them and causing productivity to suffer.

How Do You Resolve Conflicts?

When an employer is trying to find out how you interact with others, she may ask questions about hypothetical situations. For example, she may ask how you would resolve a problem with a coworker. Alternatively, the interviewer may ask you to discuss times you actually did experience conflict with another individual. You should always present a balanced look at those situations. Everyone knows there are three sides to every story—your side, the other person's side, and the truth. Instead of taking sides, try to offer a look at the situation from everyone's point of view and talk about how you effectively dealt with the problem and solved it. Just as you should avoid placing all the blame on someone else, you should also avoid taking all the blame yourself.

 Essential

A potential employer will try to find out if you are someone who either causes conflicts or doesn't know how to resolve them when they occur. If you indicate that you have a tendency to have difficulties getting along with others, it will raise a red flag and he will be less likely to hire you.

An employer may be interested in knowing how you resolve serious conflicts before they escalate. Too often we hear about an angry employee losing control and doing something to physically harm his employer or coworkers. Your prospective employer wants to know you are a calm and reasonable person who doesn't let her anger get out of hand. If you are interviewing for a supervisory position, the interviewer will want to know that you have the ability to defuse other people's anger.

Questions and Answers

Q Unfortunately, every office has personality conflicts. What do you do when you work with someone you don't particularly like?

A While I know you don't have to be buddies with all your colleagues, workplaces are more productive if everyone gets along. I would try to resolve my differences with that person. If that wasn't possible, I'd find something about that person I could admire and respect, and I'd focus on that instead of the things I didn't like.

This applicant shows he's proactive when he says he would try to work out his differences with his coworker but realistic when he says that if he can't, he will find something to respect about his coworker.

Never Say: "I get along with everyone, so this won't be a problem." Is this person too good to be true? Probably.

Q What would you do if you disagreed with your boss?

A It would depend on the situation. If I disagreed with her about whether the office is warm or cold I might not say anything. However, if I disagreed with my boss about whether the new marketing campaign was going to work, I'd share my thoughts with her.

This applicant knows he has to choose his battles wisely. There's a difference between being disagreeable and disagreeing.

Never Say: "I would never tell my boss I disagreed with her." This applicant is too passive.

Q What do you expect someone you supervise to do if she disagrees with you?

A I would expect that person to let me know what she's thinking. It could influence my decision. If she doesn't share her thoughts with me, I won't have the opportunity to hear her take on things.

This job candidate respects his coworkers' opinions. He knows it wouldn't be wise to make decisions without taking their comments into consideration.

Never Say: "Disagreeing with your supervisor? Isn't that a little disrespectful?" This candidate's answer implies that he is more interested in his own image and power than in his company's success.

Q What would you do if your supervisor handed you an assignment, but you didn't quite understand it?

A I would first make sure I didn't just need to take a closer look at the project to better understand it. Once I did that, I would ask questions if I needed to. I'd rather ask questions before I begin than have to correct mistakes later on.

This candidate tries to work independently when possible, but knows that clarification is sometimes necessary and is not afraid to ask for it.

Never Say: "I would try to figure it out on my own." This interviewee is trying to show that she is independent, but her answer may send up red flags. The employer will wonder if this independence will cause the candidate to make mistakes.

Q What would you do if your boss asks you do something that is clearly not part of your job description?

A It would depend on what it was I was asked to do. I wouldn't expect to run personal errands for my boss, but if I were asked to do something to help the company that wasn't normally part of my job, I wouldn't have a problem with it.

With this answer, the applicant shows his flexibility. However, this extends only to situations where the request is appropriate. If the boss is looking for someone to run her personal errands and that is something the candidate refuses to do, it's better to set things straight right from the start.

Never Say: "I would do anything I was asked to do." While flexibility is important, no one should be a pushover.

Q How did you get along with your last supervisor?

A We had a great relationship. I really respected him and I know he respected me, too. My supervisor knew he could trust me with any project, so he always assigned me those that were very challenging.

This candidate describes her relationship with her boss on a professional level, yet manages to say something very positive about herself.

Never Say: "We got along so well. We had lunch together all the time." It sounds like this interviewee is describing a buddy, not a supervisor.

Q What would you do if a member of your staff seemed upset about something, but you didn't know what the problem was?

A I would ask if he wanted to talk about what's bothering him and make sure he knew I was available. If he didn't want to talk I wouldn't push, because it might be something personal. However, if it were work-related, I would hope he'd be able to be honest about it so we'd be able to solve the problem together.

This candidate demonstrates both sensitivity and professionalism with this answer. She is sensitive to the needs of her staff and indicates that she is approachable, especially when it comes to work-related issues.

Never Say: "I have to maintain a distance between myself and my staff. If there's something I need to know, my employee should come to me. If it's a personal problem, he can just leave it at home where it belongs." This candidate shows that she hasn't yet developed an understanding of what it means to be a good manager.

 Alert

Employers want managers who can strike a balance between compassion and professionalism when dealing with their subordinates. They prefer managers who don't become so personally involved with their staff members that it clouds their judgment, but, at the same time, are approachable and understanding.

Q Have you ever had a boss you didn't like?

A Of course I've worked for some bosses I've liked more than others, but I try to stay professional and always make an effort to get along with everyone.

"Never complain about a former boss" is the line that keeps running through this candidate's head. Rather than do that, he keeps his answer as positive as possible.

Never Say: "Have I ever! Let me tell you about my last boss." This candidate seems eager to talk about his employer behind her back. Is that the kind of person the interviewer wants around his office?

Q What would you do if you received what you felt was an unfair evaluation?

A I would wait a little while before I approached my supervisor—probably until the next morning. I wouldn't want to talk to my supervisor while I was angry, because I might say the wrong thing. I would write down point-by-point why I thought the evaluation was inaccurate. Then I would present my thoughts to my supervisor calmly.

This candidate shows that he does not act on emotion. He takes the time to evaluate a situation before making a move. After doing that, he makes an effort to calmly present his case.

Never Say: "I'd march right into her office and tell her how wrong she is." The last thing an employer wants is an employee who acts on his emotions. A job candidate should come across as someone who thinks carefully before he acts or speaks.

Q What would you do if someone you supervised came to you because he felt your evaluation of him was unfair?

A I would ask him to explain to me why he thought the evaluation was unfair. If he had a valid argument to back up his claim, I would reconsider the evaluation. If not, I would sit down with him to discuss what improvements could be made so that his next evaluation would be better.

This interviewee illustrates how she takes the time to listen to her subordinates. She shows she is willing to make changes to the evaluation if she realizes she needs to, but if not, she will try to help the employee improve.

Never Say: "I'm really careful when I write evaluations, so they are always accurate." This job candidate doesn't realize that everyone makes mistakes, even those who are really careful.

Q Describe the ideal coworker.

A The ideal coworker is one who respects those around him. He doesn't engage in behavior that would be offensive to others. He offers constructive criticism and accepts it as well. He contributes to the department and company and doesn't try to compete with his coworkers. He shares responsibility for victories as well as defeats.

This applicant lists a number of desirable qualities and shows that he understands what makes a good employee. Hopefully, this candidate is also describing traits he possesses.

Never Say: "I prefer someone who keeps to himself. I really don't want to make friends at work." If this is what this candidate believes, he will have trouble being part of a congenial environment.

Q Describe the ideal manager.

A The ideal manager expects a lot of her employees. She respects them. She knows their individual abilities and makes sure they utilize them to the fullest. She continually challenges them to do more and recognizes their accomplishments.

This answer can mean one of two things. The candidate may be describing her own abilities as a manager. In that case, this is a manager who will retain a productive staff. Alternatively, she could be describing the type of manager she'd like to work under. If that is the case, an employee who likes to work under a supervisor who expects a lot is someone willing to live up to those expectations.

Never Say: "The ideal manager is one who doesn't interfere too much with her employees. I like someone who just lets people do their jobs." If this candidate is describing herself as a manager, she shows that she lacks managerial skills. If she is describing a manager she'd like to work for, she has shown herself as a worker who, for some reason, doesn't want anyone to know what she is doing.

Q Describe the ideal employee.

A The ideal employee is one who always does more than he is asked to do. He is open to challenges and is always willing to learn more and take on more responsibilities. He is also receptive to constructive criticism.

Hopefully this candidate has described himself, and any employer would be happy to have an employee like this.

Never Say: "The ideal employee is one who does what is asked of him. He doesn't ask a lot of questions." This candidate, if describing himself, sounds weak.

Q What would you do if someone came to you to complain about his supervisor?

A First, I would ask him if he had talked to his supervisor yet. If not, I would ask him to do that first. I would make sure he knew how to approach the supervisor and offer him tips if he didn't. If he had already talked to his supervisor but hadn't gotten anywhere with her, I would have him tell me his side of the story. Next, I would talk to his supervisor to get her side of the story. After considering what both people had told me, I would decide how to resolve the problem.

This job candidate shows he knows how to follow protocol when he says he would ask the employee to speak to his supervisor first. He demonstrates that he won't take sides and must hear both sides of a story before deciding what to do.

Never Say: "I'd listen to what he had to say and then call his supervisor down to my office so I could deal with the problem immediately." This interviewee indicates that he wastes no time, but this is not the best way to deal with a serious problem.

Q What would your current coworkers say about you?

A My coworkers would say I'm very committed to my job. I work hard to contribute to each project's success, and I always share credit with everyone else who contributes to that success.

This interviewee portrays herself as someone who is a team player. She sticks to talking about work-related matters.

Never Say: "They would say they like me." That's nice, but the applicant should try to think up something a little more concrete to show why she is a good employee.

Alert

Every work environment is different, and the interviewer wants to know if you will succeed in this one. Employers put a lot of effort into making sure they hire the most suitable candidates possible. The candidate must be able to carry out the necessary job duties, and she must fit in well with the other employees.

Q What would you do about a long-term employee whose work has been slipping lately?

A I would talk to my employee to find out what was going on. Obviously if this person always did a good job, something must have happened to change that. As a supervisor, it is my job to find out what that is and help the employee fix the problem; it is also preferable to firing someone. It is generally more cost effective to retain a worker who already knows the job than to train someone new. It also is better for the morale of that person's coworkers, who don't want to see a coworker lose his job.

This answer shows that the candidate has good managerial skills. While dismissing an unproductive employee may seem like a quick and easy solution in the short term, it can have a detrimental effect on the company in the end.

Never Say: "Whoever doesn't pull his weight has to go. I would just fire the employee." This candidate may know how to solve a problem quickly, but she doesn't account for the repercussions.

Q What would you do if an important client asked you out on a date?

A I would politely decline, explaining that I make a point of never mixing business with pleasure. I would then thank him and end the conversation as quickly as possible.

Good answer. This candidate won't compromise her integrity.

Never Say: "How important is this client?"

Q Have you ever had to persuade someone to accept your point of view? How did you do it, and were you successful?

A I have had to do that several times. A few months ago, for example, we were in the process of planning a new publication. We were deciding whether to hire a permanent employee or a freelancer to edit it. My manager felt we should go with a permanent employee. After analyzing the options, I felt strongly that hiring a freelancer would work best. I presented him with my reasons for wanting to hire a freelancer, including a cost analysis. I convinced my manager to try it my way, and so far it has worked out very well.

This interviewee gives an example that explains how she gathered information to help her make a decision and then presented the information to her manager to persuade him that this was the best choice.

Never Say: "I've had to do that several times. I can always get people to come around to my point of view." It is unclear how this candidate persuades others to come around to her point of view. Is she assertive or aggressive?

Q How do you handle an angry employee?

A Way too often you hear about an employee whose anger turns to violence. As a supervisor, it would be my job to recognize potentially volatile situations. Once I recognized a problem, I would help the employee remove herself from the situation long enough to cool down. I would tell her where she could go for help.

This applicant knows anger can be serious and what to do before it escalates.

Never Say: "I'd fire her." This applicant shows that he knows how to further escalate a potentially violent situation.

Q What do you do when you have a very unhappy customer?

A My first step is to let the customer know I will listen to what she has to say. If the company has a strict policy regarding customer complaints, I will follow it. However, if I must use my own judgment, I would strike a balance between keeping the customer happy and not costing my employer too much. If I see that the customer's complaint is legitimate, I will do what it takes to remedy the situation.

This applicant plays by the rules. He knows a satisfied customer will return, but he also realizes that a company is always concerned about its bottom line.

Never Say: "The customer is always right. I will just give a customer what they want." If every customer is right, it will cost the company a lot of money.

Q If you were unhappy with your job, how would you discuss this with your boss?

A I've always had good relationships with everyone I've worked for, so I think it would be to everyone's benefit for me to be direct with my boss. First, I would make a list of the things I'm unhappy with, as well as suggestions for improving each situation. I would then ask for a meeting with my boss to go over the list point by point, being careful not to place any blame.

This interviewee smartly points out that he maintains a good relationship with his boss that can withstand this type of discussion. He explains how he would be proactive in helping to find a solution for the problems he is dealing with at work.

Never Say: "I don't think I'd bother discussing it. I would just look for another job." This answer may indicate that this candidate makes rash decisions and may not be loyal to this job if he gets it.

 Alert

> Show that you can resolve problems on your own before you bring someone else into it. A candidate who indicates that she will go running to her supervisor to report difficulties with a coworker will be viewed by the interviewer as too high maintenance.

Q How do you handle criticism?

A I think criticism can be a valuable tool. It forces me to take a look at my own work to see how I can improve on it.

This candidate shows that she doesn't get all bent out of shape if someone has an unkind word for her.

Never Say: "If someone can't say something nice, maybe they shouldn't say anything at all."

CHAPTER 11

Did You Do Your Homework?

R esearching a prospective employer is one of the most important things you can do to prepare for a job interview. You should keep up with the latest news about a company, and find out about its line of business, financial condition, clients, and the industry in which it operates. Arriving at the interview armed with this information shows the prospective employer how serious you are about the interview and about the job.

Proving Your Knowledge

During the course of a job interview, the person conducting it will ask you to discuss what you know about her company and the particular job for which she is hiring.

A job candidate who walks into an interview armed with knowledge about the employer demonstrates several things to the interviewer. He demonstrates that he isn't just looking for a job with any employer. He wants to work for this particular company because of what he knows about it. He also shows that he was ambitious enough to do the necessary research to learn what he could about the employer.

The interviewer may ask you direct questions regarding what you know about the company. If you haven't done your research, you won't be able to answer these questions. She will ask you about the company's services and its products. She may also want you to talk about the industry of which the company is a part.

 Essential

To find basic information about a prospective employer, start by looking at the company's website. You can learn about a company's product line and key personnel. Public companies often make their annual reports available on their websites. Some also provide a list of clients.

The interviewer may also ask you questions that aren't as straightforward. You may not even realize at first that she is testing your knowledge about the company. For example, the interviewer may ask you what you can contribute to the company and what changes you would make if you were hired. She may ask you why you want to work for the company and how this opportunity fits into your career plans. Base your answers on the information you gathered through your research.

Highlight Skills That Fit the Company

Throughout a job interview, you will be asked many questions about your skills, work history, and accomplishments. The interviewer will ask you these questions because he wants to find out what you can bring to his company. The more you know about this employer, the better you can demonstrate you have the particular attributes he values. Use what you learned through your research to frame your answers. For example, if you found out the company is in the process of expanding its web presence, talk about your skills, work history, and accomplishments in that area. Your goal is to not merely talk about your attributes in general terms but to discuss them as they relate to this particular job.

Questions and Answers

Q Now that you've told me about yourself, can you tell me what you know about us?

A Costello Laboratories is a pharmaceutical company with annual sales of over $15 billion. The company recently introduced a new medication to treat bipolar disorder, and I read that it is working on a new cardiac medication.

This answer shows that this candidate has done her homework. She knows what the company does and has even kept up with the latest news.

Never Say: "I haven't been able to find out anything about it." Unless you've been called for an interview an hour before it is to take place, there is no excuse for not doing your homework.

Q What do you think it takes to be successful here?

A I understand that Q & H Corporation introduced five new products to the market in the last year alone. In order to be a successful employee of such an innovative company, one would have to be very creative. In a competitive industry like soaps and toiletries, you need employees who can keep up with what consumers want.

This person has obviously done his homework. He not only knows about the company, but he seems to know about the industry as well.

Never Say: "In order to be successful, employees must work hard and do a good job." This can be said of employees of any company. If this candidate had done his homework, he would know more about this particular company.

Q Based on what you know about this company, how will you contribute to it?

A I see that most of your company's clients are in the food industry. Since I spent ten years working for AMJ Bean Company, I am very familiar with that industry. I know my experience in the industry is something your clients will appreciate.

This candidate has researched her prospective employer and knows that her experience in the food industry will help her should she be hired. She is able to make a point of mentioning that on the job interview.

Never Say: "I have great organizational skills and I can manage my time well." While most employers value these skills, the candidate does not explain why they will benefit this particular company.

Q There are a lot of companies that can use someone with your skills. Why do you want to work at this company?

A Home Warehouse has been more successful than any other company in the hardware industry. The company has seen steady profit growth over many years, and it appears it will continue to do so. However, critics of the company are quick to point out that customer service is seriously lacking. As the director of customer service, I will implement new procedures that will turn that negative image around.

This answer shows the interviewee's knowledge of the company, including its weaknesses. He already has a plan in mind to fix that weakness, and he shares it with the interviewer.

Never Say: "I heard you pay really well." This candidate shows that he doesn't really know a lot about the company and how he will fit in as an employee.

Q Why do you want to work in this industry?

A I'm ready for a new challenge, and since more commercial banks have begun to offer investment services over the last few years, I know I can use the skills I learned as an investment banker to work in the commercial banking industry.

By giving this answer, the interviewee is able to demonstrate that he knows about this industry and what he can bring to it.

Never Say: "The hours are much better than they are in the investment banking industry." This answer doesn't show that the interviewee knows more about the industry than the number of hours one must work, and it certainly doesn't show what he can bring to it.

Q How much do you know about our company's recent growth?

A I know that XYZ Brands is a multinational company. I was particularly intrigued by your acquisition of ABC Corporation last March. It seems like it's going to open up a whole new market for this company.

Not only does the interviewee show that she took the time to learn about the company, she also shows she's kept up with the latest news about it. Notice that the interviewee said, "it's going to open up a whole new market for this company" not "your company," so as not to create distance between herself and the employer.

Never Say: "I see your commercials on TV all the time, so you must be a pretty big company."

Q What interests you about our products and services?

A Turning Corporation provides products and services that help so many people. Just the other day, I was reading about the new motorized scooter Turning developed. Those in health care and advocates for the disabled are very excited about it, according to everything I've read.

This candidate has obviously made a point of learning about his prospective employer, including keeping up with news about the latest products.

Never Say: "I don't know much about your products, but by the looks of your offices, they must sell really well."

Q Is there anything you find troubling about this industry?

A Actually, no. I've been reading a lot about this industry and everything I've seen so far is positive. This industry has made a great recovery after the decline about a decade ago. Since then it has been growing steadily and actually saw record growth last year.

Although he doesn't have anything negative to say, this candidate takes this opportunity to show that he did his homework.

Never Say: "No. It's nice to be in an industry like this, isn't it?" This interviewee may have done his homework, but he needs to elaborate on his answer to prove that.

Q Where do you think this company is going to be in five years?

A Based on what I've been reading, it seems this company will be fully expanded into the international market by then. Parker Corporation opened offices in Japan and Switzerland last year, and I read that they are looking into opening Canadian offices next year.

This candidate is aware of what her prospective employer has in store for the future because she did her homework.

Never Say: "The future is always so fuzzy. Who can ever predict what is going to happen?" This interviewer didn't ask this candidate to look into a crystal ball. He wants her to make a prediction based on her current knowledge.

Q Do you know what your job duties will be if we hire you?

A As eligibility clerk, I know I will use my interviewing skills to help determine whether individuals are eligible to receive assistance from various government programs. I will interview people and then write reports that will be sent to the appropriate agencies.

Because she looked into it, this candidate knows what the general duties are for the job.

Never Say: "I didn't get a chance to look into that." The interviewer will wonder how this candidate can interview for a job she knows nothing about.

Q How does this job fit in with your career goals?

A As I mentioned earlier, my long-range goal is to be an elementary school principal. Reaching that is several years off, of course. I have a lot to learn about school administration. I've attended several workshops you've run; I'm always impressed by your knowledge, and I know I can learn a lot from you. From what I've heard through the grapevine, you always place a lot of trust in everyone you hire and give employees a chance to grow. I know I can gain valuable knowledge and experience here at Oakwood, in addition to what I can contribute as an assistant principal.

This candidate demonstrates his knowledge about his prospective employer. He has personally learned from her in the past. He has also talked to other people who know her and how the school is run. Mentioning his aspiration to move beyond this job is a little bit risky, but since it will be quite a while before he can do that, he takes a chance.

Never Say: "It's an assistant principal job and clearly it's the next step I need to take in order to become a principal." In other words, this interviewee doesn't care where he gets his experience as long as he gets it.

Q If we hire you, what aspect of this job do you think you'll like best? What aspect of the job will you like least?

A I will enjoy working with clients one-on-one best, as I have in my previous position. The part I will like least is completing the massive quantity of paperwork that is required by all government agencies. However, I know it's a necessary part of this job and I've learned that if you keep up with it, it is much easier to deal with.

Demonstrating what she knows about the job, this candidate is able to discuss what she likes and doesn't like about it. She picks the major part of her job, working with clients, as the thing she likes best. When saying what she doesn't enjoy, she is upbeat and quick to point out that she knows it is necessary.

Never Say: "I love working with clients but I hate doing all the paperwork." It would be better for this candidate not to be so vehement about her dislike of paperwork.

Q What would you like to accomplish here if we hire you?

A I read that this company is expanding into the children's clothing market. With my background in that area, I know I can help make that clothing line successful.

The interviewee bases his answer on what he has learned about this employer. He explains how his experience will help the company reach its goals.

Never Say: "I hope to move up to the executive suite." The candidate may have researched the layout of the office to determine that this suite exists, but that's not exactly the type of research that will impress a prospective employer.

Q Since all your experience has been in another industry, you must be a little concerned about making this change. What do you think working in this industry will be like?

A Everything in this industry seems to go at a very fast pace. I think the transition will be an easy one for me because in the magazine industry, I also worked at a fast pace. There were tight deadlines and sudden changes that needed to be dealt with on a moment's notice. From what I can tell, this industry involves the same things. I think I will be able to make a seamless transition to this industry.

This candidate's answer conveys that she has some knowledge of the company's industry, and she feels she can adapt to working in it.

Never Say: "I think it will be fine." This candidate needs to explain why she feels that way.

Q What do you know about some of our major clients?

A I know your major clients are all in the canned food industry. BBR represents Heller Foods, Green Products, and Acorn Corp. I read in Advertising Digest just last week that Heans hired you to run their new broadcast campaign.

This candidate has done his homework, even keeping up with the latest industry news.

Never Say: "I haven't had a chance to find out who they are." There is never an excuse for not attempting to learn what you can about a prospective employer.

Q Describe your ideal job.

A Ideally, I'd like to work as a senior project manager overseeing the development of housing complexes.

Through her research, this candidate has learned the job for which she is interviewing will eventually lead to the one she is describing. She demonstrates that she will be loyal to the company if it hires her.

Never Say: "I'd love to teach one day." It's nice to have career aspirations, but they should at least be related to the job you are applying for.

 Essential

When a prospective employer asks you to describe your dream job, choose one on your career path. You don't want to describe a job that is unrelated to the one for which you are applying. The job you describe should also be several rungs above your current one on the career ladder. Show how you want your career to progress.

Q Describe your ideal company to work for.

A I'd like to work for a software company where I will have the opportunity to contribute to the business by utilizing my programming skills as well as my teaching abilities.

When describing his ideal company, this applicant speaks in terms of what he can bring to it. Any company is ideal to him if he can use his skills to benefit it, he seems to be saying. Having done his homework, he knows he is describing the company at which he is interviewing.

Never Say: "I'd really like to work for a big company, but none of them are hiring right now." Honesty isn't always the best policy.

Q Our latest venture has been all over the news. What would you do to make the transition go more smoothly for our employees?

A I would make sure employees know how the merger between this company and Pacific Pencil Company will affect them. I would hold meetings to discuss how procedures will change and schedule workshops to help employees adapt to these changes. When my former employer merged with RQR International, I assisted the vice president who was responsible for handling the transition, so I have experience in this area.

By referring to the venture by name, this candidate shows she knows what the interviewer is talking about. She has clearly given some thought to how this merger will affect the company and knows how to deal with it, and she draws upon her experience with a similar situation.

Never Say: "What venture is that? I haven't had time lately to pay attention to the news."

 ## Question

What should I do if I don't know much about the job for which I'm applying?
Sometimes employers release little information about open positions. If the interviewer asks you what you know about the job but you haven't managed to find many details, say so. You can tell her what you know so far and use this opportunity to ask for a better description.

Q Can you define this position as you understand it?

A This position involves supervising a staff of about fifty-five data entry clerks. I would be responsible for scheduling employees, delegating work assignments, and quality control.

This candidate understands the job for which he is interviewing. He has read the job announcement and has listened carefully during the interview.

Never Say: "Data entry supervisor." It's good that the candidate at least knows the title of the job he is interviewing for. However, it's not good enough. He needs to elaborate if possible.

Q Are you available during the hours we're open?

A Yes, I am. I took a look at your website and saw that the library provides service Monday through Saturday from 9 A.M. to 9 P.M. I'm available during all those times.

This interviewee knows what the hours are and can commit to working when he is needed.

Never Say: "What hours are you open?" The candidate should have been able to find this information.

Q You are aware you will have to relocate to this city if we hire you. Do you think you will like living here?

A I've done some research about this city, and I think it would be a great place to live. The crime rate is pretty low and the climate is just about perfect. There are so many museums and theaters here, it won't be hard to find something to do on my time off.

This answer proves that this candidate has done her research and learned as much as she could about this city. She is prepared to make a well-informed decision if the employer offers her the job.

Never Say: "I can be happy anywhere." This interviewee may show that she is flexible, but since she didn't do any research into moving to a new location, this prospective employer may not see her as someone who is committed to making a permanent move.

 Alert

An employer should not ask if you are unable to work on a particular day due to religious observance. The Civil Rights Act of 1964 prohibits employment discrimination on the basis of religion. If you can't work on a particular day, hold off on having this discussion until you have received a job offer.

Q Do you know who our major competitors are?

A Yes, I do. There are four big names in the communications industry. There's BCD, DRG, Parrot, and of course, this company, Chime.

This candidate couldn't have answered this question had she not done her homework.

Never Say: "Nope."

Q Would you rather be a big fish in a small pond or a small fish in a big pond?

A I would much rather be a big fish in a small pond. Working for a small company provides me with the opportunity to use more of my skills. I like it when my job duties are diversified. Most of my experience has been with small companies, so I understand the unique challenges that can come up. For example, I know how to be careful when scheduling out-of-town business meetings so there are always enough people in the office to deal with emergencies that come up.

This candidate is interviewing for a job in a small company. He explains why this is a better fit for him.

Never Say: "Whichever." This candidate should use this opportunity to explain why he is a good fit for this employer.

Q What do you think will be different about working for this company than working for your current employer?

A My current employer sells home furnishings, while this company sells office furnishings. This means I will work with a different group of clients and new products; however, I can utilize my skills as a decorator and as a salesperson here as I do with my current employer.

This candidate knows enough about her prospective employer to answer this question. She makes a point of discussing how her skills can be used to work with a different product and different clientele.

Never Say: "It's a much shorter commute." This may be true, but it doesn't really have much to do with what this candidate can bring to her prospective employer.

Q How well do you understand our mission?

A From my research, I understand your mission is to develop high-quality toys that enhance learning and provide entertainment for children between preschool and ten years of age.

This candidate states the company's mission as he understands it, which is exactly what the interviewer asked him to do.

Never Say: "Well . . . I know you sell toys." While you may not always be able to find out what a company's mission is, you should at least try to do the research.

Q If you were interviewing potential employees for a job here, how would you describe this organization to them?

A XRT, Inc. manufactures windows and sells them directly to the consumer. The company has a sales force of about twenty people who respond to customer inquiries by visiting their homes or places of business.

This answer shows that this interviewee has a firm grasp of what this business is all about.

Never Say: "It's a window company in Chicago." This answer doesn't prove this candidate knows much about this company.

CHAPTER 12

What Would You Do If You Were Hired?

When a prospective employer looks at you, she sees you in three ways—past, present, and future. Your work history and your education make up your past. Your personality, strengths and weaknesses, and skills make up your present, or who you are today. Finally, a prospective employer wants to know the future—that is, what you would do if she hires you. Without a crystal ball, she must ask a lot of questions in order to get a clearer picture of who you are.

What You Can Bring to the Company

The interviewer's primary concern is to find out if you will be able to carry out the duties of the job. Usually you will have had the opportunity to read a job description in advance. If not, try your best to determine what the typical job duties are. You should be ready to explain why you are qualified to carry out each one.

A prospective employer might talk about some specific projects he has in store for his new hire. He will want you to discuss how you will approach those projects. This would be a good time for you to talk about how you approached similar projects in the past. The interviewer may also present a number of hypothetical situations and ask you to explain how you will handle them. When possible, draw on your past experiences to illustrate how your skills will enable you to deal with each one.

 Essential

Arm yourself with a cache of examples that best illustrate why you are the most qualified candidate for the job. These examples will come from your work experience or, in lieu of that, from your experience as a student, whether in class or through your participation in extracurricular activities.

What the Company Expects of You

Every employer has different expectations for her employees. While one might require you to work long hours on a regular basis, another might expect you to work late occasionally, perhaps during a particular busy season. Some jobs involve frequent travel. For other jobs you must be on call during weekends. The interviewer will try to determine whether you can meet a particular job requirement by asking you direct and indirect questions about it.

It is in your best interest to be honest about what you are willing to do regarding traveling and working late. If you know you must pay your dues and will be amenable to doing whatever your boss asks of you, then by all means indicate that during the interview. However, if you are not, you should let the employer know right away. It is always best to be up front and not create false expectations.

A job interview is about more than the employer deciding if he should hire you. You can use the information you gather to decide whether the company is a good fit for you. You will be able to learn about the demands of the job from some of the interviewer's questions. You may uncover a deal-breaker that was not mentioned in the job description. For example, when an interviewer asks if working late is a problem for you, it indicates the employer will probably expect you to do that. If you can't or don't want to, this is probably not a good place for you to work. You should consider yourself lucky to have learned this now rather than further along in the hiring process, or even worse, after you have accepted a job offer. If extenuating circumstances prevent you from fulfilling a certain job requirement—for example, if you can't work late because of another obligation but can come in early and are willing to do so—let the interviewer know. Your prospective employer may be able to work within the parameters of your schedule.

 Alert

If an interviewer asks about your ability to travel or work late, saying you can't do it will probably take you out of the running. Speak up only if you're sure you're not able or willing. However, if you don't speak up during the interview, you must do so before accepting a job offer.

In addition to trying to learn what you will bring to the company, a prospective employer may also want to find out what you expect to get from it, particularly your salary requirements. If possible, avoid discussing salary during a job interview, or at least during a first interview. That topic is best put off until you are closer to receiving an offer. If the interviewer asks what salary you are looking for, attempt to turn the question around on him by asking what salary the company is offering. If that doesn't work, talk about the typical salary range in your field, leaving an extensive discussion of specifics for later.

Questions and Answers

Q The department you would be in charge of hasn't had a supervisor in months. This is going to be a big transition for the staff. How will you handle it?

A I wouldn't want to make any big changes for at least the first two weeks. I find it's better to just observe how things are done before trying to make any improvements. I want to gain the staff's trust first and listen to their concerns.

This candidate has a plan in place and she lays it out step by step. She knows that employees who have been unsupervised for a long time need to get used to having someone overseeing their work.

Never Say: "Well, the first thing I would do is make some changes around here. If there hasn't been a supervisor running things for a while, things are sure to be messed up." This is not a well-thought-out answer and could indicate that the applicant might make impulsive decisions.

Q The person who fills this position will have to work on his own most of the time. Can you handle that?

A I am used to working independently. On my last job, I edited the company newsletter. I was responsible for compiling the material, writing the articles, and preparing the newsletter for publication each quarter. I had to set my own deadlines for each step along the way.

This candidate explains how a project he was responsible for prepared him to work independently.

Never Say: "I love working on my own. It's less distracting." This answer shows that this candidate may be able to work on his own, but he's inflexible. If he had to work with others, could he?

Q How do you feel about working long hours?

A Can you explain what you mean by long hours? Does that mean working late or getting to work early?

The applicant knows she already has a commitment two nights a week. She doesn't mind getting to work early, though. She decides it's better to find out what her prospective employer's expectations are before she rules anything out or commits to something with which she won't be able to follow through.

Never Say: "I love working long hours. It means I don't have to go home and deal with my family." Even if the applicant is trying to be funny, this is not the place to bring up personal issues.

 Question

What should I do if I don't understand a question?
If you don't understand what the interviewer is asking you or you just need something clarified, it's okay to ask questions during the interview. It is preferable to giving a response that doesn't answer the question.

Q We're kind of casual here. I see you've worn a suit today. How would you dress for work if I hire you?

A I would adhere to the culture of this company and dress in slacks and a nice shirt.

This candidate knows it's important to fit in with the culture of the workplace. Only after a quick assessment of the interviewer's attire does he go on with the second part of his answer.

Never Say: "I feel more comfortable in a suit." Perhaps he would feel more comfortable elsewhere.

Q Senior citizens represent a huge market now, and we want to convince them to buy our product. If we hired you, how would you help with that?

A In addition to being a very big market, the senior market is also a growing market. They are a group with a very active lifestyle. Many have expendable income and they choose to use their savings on travel, so it's clear we have a product they will want. We have to determine how to reach them. I would first do research to find out what publications seniors read and what television shows they watch. Only then can we embark on an advertising campaign.

This candidate demonstrates the methodical approach she would take. She shows her understanding of the market.

Never Say: "Seniors don't have a lot of money to spend, so why would we target them?" This interviewee doesn't know the market and contradicts the interviewer.

Q We're about to change over to a new software program for our shipping and receiving department. We'd like the person we hire for this position to do the training. Are you the right person for that job?

A I am definitely the right person for this job. As you can see on my resume, my last job was with a software distributor. One of my responsibilities was to travel to our clients' offices to provide software training.

This is one confident candidate who clearly illustrates he has the skills the company is seeking.

Never Say: "Um, I did some training." This applicant doesn't sound very confident.

Q In about a year we want to open a new branch on the other side of town. We plan to train the person who takes this position to run that office. Is that something you'd be interested in?

A I would welcome that opportunity if it arises.

Notice the applicant says, "If it arises." She wants to express her eagerness to take on more responsibility with this employer without sounding like she'd leave if that opportunity doesn't come up, or if such an opportunity comes up sooner with another company.

Never Say: "That's exactly what I'm looking for." Since the candidate only just learned of these plans, how can a job running a new but currently nonexistent office be exactly what she's looking for? What about the job for which she's currently interviewing?

Q If we hire you, will you be willing to get your certification? You have all the skills we're looking for, but we really need someone who is certified.

A I was planning to take my certification exam in June. That's the next time it's being given.

While it would have been okay for this candidate to say he would get his certification because the prospective employer has asked him to, it's even better that he said he was planning to do it anyway.

Never Say: "I don't understand why certification matters so much, but if you need me to do it, I will." Show some enthusiasm, please.

Q The person who last held this position took ill and has only been able to work off and on for the last three months. Last month he resigned. Things are a huge mess, which the person we hire will need to sort out. Are you up for the challenge?

A I love a good challenge. First I'll sort through the mess to organize it. Then I'll see which things require immediate attention and which things I can work on later.

The interviewee, by giving this answer, shows that she knows how to both organize and prioritize. These are two skills that are extremely important for someone taking over a job that has been neglected.

Never Say: "I'm sure once I see the mess, I'll figure out what to do with it." Even though this candidate shows confidence, she doesn't present a plan.

Q The person we hire will have to respond to customer complaints occasionally. Will you be able to do that?

A Years ago I worked in customer service. I'll be able to put that experience to good use.

The interviewee finds some past experience that will help him with this aspect of the job.

Never Say: "I'm sure it won't be too big a deal." If the interviewer bothered to ask this question, it may, in fact, be a big deal.

Q We often work on teams here. Would you rather work on a team or on your own?

A I work well both independently and on a team. In my previous jobs I had to do both. We often worked on teams to complete larger projects. I like how working on a team allows you to draw on the strength of each of its members.

This interviewee shows she is flexible enough to work on either a team or independently but addresses the focus of the question by emphasizing her teamwork skills.

Never Say: "On a team, of course." This candidate just says what she thinks the interviewer wants to hear without giving any proof to back up her answer.

Q We have several clients with outstanding bills. If we hire you, how will you handle this situation?

A First, I would want to go through the paperwork to make sure these clients were properly notified that their accounts are delinquent. If I find out they were notified, I'll call each one personally to discuss this. There might be extenuating circumstances. It's important not to be too heavy-handed in dealing with these types of situations. After all, these are our clients. We don't want to lose them entirely.

This candidate gives a clearly thought-out answer illustrating that he knows how important it is to be diplomatic when dealing with clients.

Never Say: "My first priority would be getting on the phone and getting payment from them as quickly as possible." While this might work, it would also alienate clients.

Q Our clients expect a very quick turnaround on the projects we do for them. Can you handle that?

A Yes, I can. While I was in graduate school, I had several professors who assigned projects that were due only a few days later. I became an expert at scheduling my time around completing these assignments.

Since this interviewee doesn't have work experience to draw upon, she talks about her experience as a student. In the process she highlights a valuable skill—time management.

Never Say: "I'm sure I can." This interviewee needs to give a specific example or, in the absence of one, talk about any skills she possesses that will help her.

Q If you are hired for this position, you will go from managing your current staff of ten to managing fifty people. Will you be able to oversee a substantially larger staff?

A Yes, I will. Although I've never managed a staff of that size before, I know I have the skills necessary to do it. I am a strong leader. I am good at communicating with my staff so that each member knows what he or she needs to accomplish. I am also adept at delegating responsibilities, which will be even more important with such a large staff.

This candidate lets the interviewer know that he has all the skills that a good manager should have, even though he doesn't have experience with the exact situation he will face.

Never Say: "Since I've never managed such a big staff, I might find it overwhelming. I'm sure I'll be able to handle it, though." This interviewee focuses on the negative rather than on why he can handle the job despite his lack of experience. He should never mention feeling overwhelmed.

Q We're implementing a new computer system in this department. If we hire you for this position, you'll need to spend a month in Seattle learning how to use it. Are you okay with that?

A That would be fine.

This is a yes or no question. The interviewee doesn't need to say any more than this. However, if the answer is "no" she will need to provide an explanation.

Never Say: "That sounds great, but do you know when that would be? It rains a lot in Seattle and I hate the rain. Don't you?" This candidate has said way too much.

Q When we are in the process of developing a new product, it's essential that information about it doesn't leak out. How are you at keeping secrets?

A After working in the technology field for the last three years, I know how important it is to keep information confidential until a product is released.

This candidate demonstrates that confidentiality has not been a problem for him in the past.

Never Say: "Wouldn't I have to sign a confidentiality agreement or something?" Is the threat of being sued for breach of contract the only thing that would keep this applicant quiet?

Q We currently have several employees who have problems with things like tardiness and excessive personal phone calls. How would you deal with this if we hired you as supervisor?

A First I would need to find out exactly what is happening. Then, prior to singling out any one employee, I would circulate a memo to the entire department that reiterated the rules. If the behavior continued, I would have a private meeting with each employee who isn't following the rules. I would stress the importance of following the rules and try to find out if there are extenuating circumstances that could be remedied. If the employee continues to break the rules, there would be repercussions.

This interviewee is clearly not one to leap without looking. She knows how important it is to evaluate a situation before taking action. However, she will take action in an expedient manner.

Never Say: "You won't have to worry about anyone breaking the rules once I take over." This candidate must put forth a series of steps she will take to remedy the situation.

Q Four times a year, we work around the clock for about a week. Will that be a problem?

A That's fine with me. I understand the beginning of each season is a very busy time.

Not only is this job candidate willing to work late, he knows enough about the industry to know what times of year this would be expected of him.

Never Say: "Do you let people take vacation during those times?" He hasn't even started and he sounds like he's trying to wiggle out of responsibility.

Q As my assistant, could you be trusted to take over for me whenever I'm out of the office?

A Absolutely. I would follow whatever rules you set forth. I also have excellent judgment, so I can handle whatever comes up.

The applicant uses this opportunity to highlight her skills.

Never Say: "Does that happen a lot?" This answer makes the applicant seem unsure of whether she can handle this responsibility.

Q Whoever fills this position will need to write next year's budget, which needs to be 10 percent lower than the current one. Could you do this?

A I had to do something similar when my department went through funding cuts last year and I was in charge of writing the new budget. First I reviewed the current year's budget and removed amounts that had been budgeted for one-time events. Then I found a few areas where our actual expenditures were lower than we had budgeted for, and I was able to bring the amount down to more realistic levels, of course accounting for possible price increases. Finally, I went through it to see what cuts would have a minimal effect on services. I cut a program that traditionally had very low attendance. This eliminated the need to hire a part-time instructor. I was able to submit a budget that was 12 percent lower than the one for the previous year.

This candidate demonstrates how he takes a practical approach to trimming a budget. He shows how he is able to get the job done with a minimal effect on service.

Never Say: "Some of the budget cuts I make may be unpopular, but saving the agency money is my priority." It's true that saving money is important. However, there are consequences of making radical cuts that will affect service.

Q This job requires some travel. Is that a problem?

A I understand that traveling is common in this industry, and that's fine with me. I look forward to representing this company around the country.

This candidate has done her homework and wisely speaks of herself as if she has the job.

Never Say: "I love traveling. There are so many places I want to visit." This candidate's mistake is talking about how she will benefit from traveling rather than talking about how her trips will benefit her prospective employer.

Q The students in this school can be very challenging to manage. As a teacher here, will you be able to handle them?

A I worked with special-needs children when I was an assistant teacher at Ardsley School. I learned it is important to look at each child as an individual. Each one has different strengths and weaknesses. If you look at it that way, you can figure out what strategy you need to use to work with each child. Children will trust you when they know you see them as individuals and will usually respond by doing what you need them to do.

Although this candidate is applying for his first professional job, he is able to draw on past experience. He explains what he learned from his previous experience as an assistant teacher.

Never Say: "I'm a strict disciplinarian, so this won't be a problem." This answer doesn't demonstrate that this interviewee has a strategy for dealing with difficult children.

Q Anyone who takes this position will need to handle stress well. Are you good at handling stress?

A Yes, I am. My last job was very stressful, but I found that practicing some relaxation techniques like deep breathing helped me combat the stress. I also made sure to take a lunch break every day, since that gives me time to regroup and start the rest of my day with a positive attitude.

This candidate demonstrates that she has strategies in place to help her deal with stress.

Never Say: "If you love your job, you don't find it stressful." That is unrealistic. Even if you love your job, it can be stressful at times. Those who have a coping mechanism will be better able to deal with stressful situations.

Q In this fast-paced environment, we need someone who can think on his feet. Are you that person?

A Yes, I am. I have experience making thoughtful decisions under pressure. I worked at a daily newspaper for five years. Every day we had to make last-minute decisions about what to include in the next day's edition. There was no time to waste when the paper had to go to press within the next half-hour.

This candidate shows how his experience has taught him how to be decisive.

Never Say: "Uhm . . . well, let me think about this. . . . Let's see . . . hmm . . ." This candidate's hesitation says more than any answer could.

Q Each employee in this department is on call one weekend a month. How do you feel about that?

A That is fine with me.

The candidate gives a succinct answer, which is all that is needed here.

Never Say: "Would I get paid for being on call?" That question can wait until a job offer is made and salary is negotiated.

Q Are you willing to work late occasionally?

A I know what it's like when a deadline is coming up. In my last job, I was asked to work late from time to time. It was never a problem for me. When a deadline is quickly approaching, I'll be able to make sure we meet it.

By giving this answer, the interviewee not only uses language that lets the interviewer visualize her in the position for which she's interviewing, but also tells her prospective boss that she's worked late in the past.

Never Say: "I'll work late every night if you want me to." Is this interviewee just saying what she thinks the interviewer wants to hear?

Question

What should I do if I can't work on a particular day because of my religious beliefs?
If you can't work on a particular day because of your religious beliefs, tell your prospective employer you'd be happy to make up the time on another day. Remember, an employer must reasonably accommodate employees' sincerely held religious beliefs and cannot base a hiring decision on this.

Q It's getting too expensive to operate a business in this city. Would you be willing to relocate?

A I'd be willing to relocate anywhere within the United States.

This candidate gives an honest answer.

Never Say: "I love to move around, so that's really good news." This applicant's answer alludes to the fact that stability isn't his strong suit.

Q What salary are you looking for?

A From my research, I know the salary range for those with my experience working in this industry here in New York is $51,000 to $55,000 per year. I'm confident we can agree on a salary that is acceptable.

This applicant has done her homework. She gives a range rather than an absolute number, showing her flexibility.

Never Say: "I have to make $52,000 per year." One should always avoid giving an absolute number when discussing salary on a job interview.

Q I see from the salary history you sent that you were earning $45,000 on your last job. We've taken some losses over the last year and won't be able to pay you that. Will that be a problem?

A I'm sure we can agree on a reasonable salary.

This applicant knows it's better to discuss salary after the employer makes an offer.

Never Say: "How much less than that will it be?" Don't make the employer think you're only in it for the money. The salary discussion should wait until later.

CHAPTER 13

Difficult or Embarrassing Questions

Do you dread going on job interviews because you are afraid the interviewer will ask you about a situation you find embarrassing or difficult to explain? Were you fired from your last job, or is there a huge gap in your work history? The interviewer is likely to notice any gaps or inconsistencies on your resume, so you need to be prepared to answer the questions of which you are most afraid. Here are strategies for coping with that aspect of job interviewing.

I Hope They Don't Ask Me That

When a prospective employer reviews your resume, he will look for things like lengthy gaps between jobs or jobs that don't fit in with the rest of your experience. He will also notice if you hopped around from job to job, or if you had a series of jobs that didn't move in an upward direction. An employer will probably question why you were at a job for a short period of time; or he may question why you have been with one employer for your entire career.

An interviewer may ask questions about your lack of experience if he feels you haven't been in the field for very long. If you appear to be overqualified for the job, the interviewer will question you about that as well. If you don't have the formal education that is called for, you will probably be asked to explain why. If your education is in one area and the job you are interviewing for is in another, the interviewer will inquire about that too.

How to Answer Difficult Questions

When you answer difficult questions, be honest. Don't make excuses for things, and do not lie. For example, if you got fired from a job, don't tell the interviewer you quit. She can learn the truth from a simple call to your former employer or through a background check, so you are better off being up front no matter how embarrassed you feel. The interviewer will appreciate your candor. If you lie, you will have two strikes against you. Not only will a prospective employer know you got fired, but you will have shown her you are dishonest. Don't place blame on your former employer or speak negatively about him. When possible, highlight the positive and talk about what you have done to overcome whatever it is that put a blemish on your past.

 Essential

An interviewer will ask you to discuss things he can't ascertain from reading your resume. While your resume gives the period of time you worked at every job, it doesn't show why you left each one. A prospective employer will want to know about that. He may also ask you to discuss your relationships with supervisors and coworkers.

If an employer asks about a gap in employment, be honest about why it's there. Discuss things you did during that time to enhance your skills. For example, if you took time off to be at home with young children, talk about how you kept up with your career by reading professional literature and taking classes. If you didn't give much thought to your career during that time, or have decided to enter a new field, talk about how you are preparing now for your return to work.

Address concerns about your lack of education or experience by explaining what you've done to compensate for it. If your experience makes up for not having a college degree, say so. If you plan to take some courses to enhance your skills, elaborate on that. Be specific when you discuss your plans.

If you were fired from a previous job, you may be concerned that revealing it will take you out of the running for a job. Regardless of that, don't try to hide it. The prospective employer will probably want to talk to your prior boss before she hires you. She will learn the truth anyway.

 Question

The word "fired" sounds so bad. Is there something I can say instead?
You don't have to use the word "fired" to say you had to leave a job. It has a negative connotation, as does "terminated" or "dismissed." You can say you had a "parting of the ways" or a "disagreement," which basically means the same thing but doesn't sound as harsh.

If you have been job hunting for a while, you are probably concerned that a prospective employer will wonder why. You can blame the economy if it's currently bad. Even if the general economy is good, the market for someone with your skills may not be. Make sure the market really is bad; you don't want to infer that you don't understand the industry. State your skills and say that you haven't been able to find a job where they are needed.

Questions and Answers

Q You were at your last job for only six months. Why were you there for such a short time?

A Unfortunately, the job turned out to be much different from what I thought it would be. It's a good thing I discovered this early on, before the employer invested more time in me and I invested more time in the company. I know I could put my editing skills to much better use in this position.

Notice the interviewer places no blame on either himself or his employer. He doesn't say the employer didn't tell him the truth about the job or that he misunderstood what he'd be doing. He also shows how he looked out for both his employer and himself by leaving before more time was invested.

Never Say: "My boss blatantly lied to me during the interview. The job turned out to be very different from what she told me." This candidate's mistake is speaking poorly of his boss.

 Alert

> Keep your negativity in check when you talk about a former employer. No matter how much you hate him, keep your feelings to yourself. Speak poorly of your former boss and a prospective employer will wonder if someday you will speak poorly of her.

Q I see from your resume that you've had five jobs in five years. Why have you moved around so much?

A When I first graduated from college, I wasn't sure what I wanted to do. After trying out several jobs, I have come to the conclusion that this field is the right one for me. I even took some courses to enhance my skills. I know I can do a good job here.

This is an honest answer. The candidate states that she has figured out what she wants to do and is now committed to this field. She then goes on to prove it by talking about how she is enhancing her skills.

Never Say: "I can't stay in one place for too long. . . . I mean, I couldn't stay in one place too long. Now I can." The candidate can't keep her answer straight. Is her need to move around still a problem? This interviewer is sure to be suspicious.

Q You've been out of the job market for the last six years. Can you explain that, please?

A I took a hiatus from the workforce to raise my children. I am now ready to come back and use my skills. I have kept up with developments in the field during my absence by reading professional literature and attending seminars.

This candidate doesn't make excuses for his time away from the workforce. He does make a point of letting the employer know he didn't lose track of his career during this time.

Never Say: "I was busy raising my family, but I can't afford to stay home anymore." This doesn't let the employer know that this candidate is ready to return to the workforce and wants to do that, only that he needs to. The interviewer will wonder if this candidate will stop working should his financial situation change.

Q According to your resume, you were a manager at Crane Computer Store from 1990 through 1995 and then assistant manager at a different branch of the store starting in 1995. Were you demoted?

A This wasn't a demotion. I was originally manager of the paper products department. It was a very small section. When an opening came up for an assistant manager in the home PC department at another store, I jumped at the chance. It was a much better opportunity because it was a much larger department and I knew I would have greater responsibilities.

Although her job title would indicate this candidate had been demoted, she explains why this wasn't actually the case. She was willing to trade the manager title for a job with more responsibility. If she had been demoted, however, she would need to explain why.

Never Say: "I didn't want all the responsibility of being a manager." Should this candidate really say she doesn't want a job with responsibility?

Q Why did you leave Community Publications Corporation?

A My boss and I had a difference of opinion, and we decided it would be best if I left my job.

The interviewee decides to be honest about his reasons for leaving his job. He doesn't blame his boss or berate himself, but simply tells the truth about being fired.

Never Say: "That idiot fired me." Making disparaging comments about your boss is a poor choice.

Q Tell me how your career progressed at your last job.

A I was hired as assistant to the staff accountant. When she left, I was asked to take her position. After three months, my boss and I decided that I didn't yet have the skills for such a demanding job after all, and I stepped back into the assistant position when they hired someone with more experience. That was three years ago, and I now have the experience I needed back then.

The candidate gives an honest answer. He explains that his "backward" progress from accountant to assistant was due to his lack of experience. He claims that he now has the experience to be a staff accountant.

Never Say: "They promoted me before I was ready and then when they found someone they liked better, they sent me back to my original job." This answer makes the candidate sound very bitter about what happened. He also doesn't say anything about the skills he currently has.

Q If I asked your previous supervisor for a reference, how would she describe you?

A My supervisor and I often disagreed about many things. One thing we would agree on, I think, is that I did my job well.

This candidate is in a tricky situation. He and his supervisor didn't get along well, but that doesn't mean he wasn't a good employee. He gives this answer hoping his former boss will put their differences aside and be honest about his performance at work if she is called as a reference.

Never Say: "She probably wouldn't have anything nice to say. She'd always had it in for me." This candidate doesn't give his supervisor a chance to say something bad about him—he does it himself.

Q Your resume says that you are an administrative assistant, yet you're applying for a job that has much more responsibility. What makes you think you can handle it?

A Even though my job title is administrative assistant, I have many more responsibilities than that title usually implies. I train all new support staff and supervise junior clerks.

This answer explains how this candidate's responsibilities differed from what one might assume from her job title. She chooses to discuss the aspects of her current job that are related to the job for which she is interviewing.

Never Say: "Even though I was technically an administrative assistant, I did a lot of other stuff." The candidate needs to be more specific and explain what that "other stuff" was in order to demonstrate she has experience handling the responsibilities she would have on the job for which she is interviewing.

Q You seem to be overqualified for this position. Why do you want this job?

A I definitely bring a lot of skills to this job. I look forward to using my experience to help your company grow.

Rather than downplay his skills in response to what the interviewer has said, this candidate chooses to talk about how his experience and skills will benefit the company.

Never Say: "I don't really have that much experience." A job candidate should never make less of his skills, regardless of what the interviewer thinks.

Q There's a ten-year gap in your employment history. What were you doing during that time?

A I was convicted of theft and was incarcerated at the state penitentiary from 1989 through 1999. During that time, I earned a degree in social work that I want to use in working with young people who may be headed in the wrong direction.

A conviction will show up when the employer does a background check on this candidate, so it makes no sense for her to lie. She makes a point of discussing why she is qualified for the job for which she has applied.

Never Say: "I took some time off from the workforce." The employer may hire the candidate in spite of a prior conviction, especially if she shows that she has turned her life around. However, if she lies about the conviction and the employer finds out the truth, she probably won't get the job.

Q Have you ever been convicted of a felony?

A Yes, I have. I served three years for a hit and run. I finished my college courses while I was in jail.

This candidate gives an honest answer and hopes it won't affect his chances of being hired. Generally, the interviewer can ask if a job candidate has ever been convicted of a felony.

Never Say: "Why? Are you going to do a background check?" The employer will certainly do a background check after hearing that response, or she may simply decide to take this candidate out of consideration for the job.

Q In your first job out of college you worked as a receptionist. Weren't you a little overqualified?

A My education did overqualify me for that job, but I was determined to work in the advertising industry. I knew if I took that job, it would give me the chance to show off my skills. I volunteered to do some proofreading for the copywriter, and after six months he asked me to be his assistant.

This candidate shows the interviewer that she knew what she had to do to reach her goals. She also tells the interviewer that her plan worked.

Never Say: "It was the only thing available." This applicant did not have a clear goal in mind when she took the job.

Q On your resume you indicated that you attended Harkin College for a few years, but I don't see a degree listed. Did you graduate?

A No, I didn't graduate. I withdrew from the college during my junior year. I decided that I wasn't getting as much out of college as I should have, so I decided to go to work. I plan to continue my education in the future.

This is an honest answer. The candidate takes responsibility for discontinuing his formal education and expresses his desire to complete his education.

Never Say: "The school was horrible. I didn't want to waste my parents' money." If this was the real reason this job candidate dropped out of school, he probably would have finished his education elsewhere.

Q What were your grades like in college?

A My grades could have been better. If I had it to do over again, I would have studied a lot harder than I did.

The candidate doesn't blame anyone but herself for her poor grades and makes a point of saying she would do things differently now.

Never Say: "They were okay." If the candidate did poorly in school she should admit it. If the employer asks for a copy of her college transcript, which he might, the candidate will be caught in a lie. Furthermore, having described her poor grades as "okay," the interviewer may question why the applicant's expectations are so low she thinks earning bad grades is okay.

Q If we hire you, the person who will be your supervisor is much younger than you are. Will this be a problem for you?

A If she has the skills necessary to be a supervisor, I will be happy to work for her.

This candidate gives a straightforward answer to this question. He does not know whether the interviewer is concerned about whether he will not be able to take direction from someone younger than he or if the interviewer is implying the candidate is too old for the job. The applicant chooses to ignore the implication that he is too old and instead addresses the interviewer's concern about his ability to take direction from a younger supervisor.

Never Say: "Are you implying that I'm old?" The candidate is much too confrontational, which will turn the interviewer off regardless of what her question implies.

Q I see you left your last job about eight months ago. Can you explain that, and have you been looking for work since then?

A Yes, I have been looking for a job for the last several months. I am skilled in technical support, system design and implementation, and training. I haven't been able to find a position for someone with my skills.

This candidate gives an honest answer to the question. He states his skills and then explains that the job market has been tight for someone with those skills. Since he has no control over the job market, he doesn't have to make excuses for it.

Never Say: "I know if I had looked harder for a job, I would have found one. After all, I have great skills." The candidate may think it's better to say he couldn't find a job because he wasn't looking for one, but this answer only shows his lack of motivation.

Q Why are you applying for a job outside the subject in which you majored?

A I can use the skills I developed as a psychology major to succeed in marketing research. I have taken courses in consumer behavior, statistics, and research design, which I know will be useful in this field.

This candidate shows how her skills are transferable to this field. If she plans to further pursue a career in psychology, she doesn't imply it by giving this answer.

Never Say: "I need to work to save up money for graduate school." The employer has good reason to wonder how long this person will stay if he hires her.

Q You don't seem to have a great deal of work experience. Why should we hire you?

A I may not have a lot of paid work experience, but I have a lot of volunteer experience. I organized a voter registration drive in my community and registered 300 new voters during the last election.

For the past four years I have chaired the committee that runs the book fair at my son's school, and we have raised more than $7,000 each year.

While this candidate doesn't have paid work experience, she has been able to hone her skills through her volunteer work. She has persuaded people to register to vote and worked on a committee that successfully ran a major fundraising event. She even gives dollar amounts to back up her claims.

Never Say: "I really want this job, and I know I will be good at it." This candidate needs to tell the interviewer what skills she has and how she will use them to benefit his company.

Q Aren't you underqualified for this job?

A I don't think I am. While it's true I don't have a lot of experience yet, I do have very good skills, as we discussed earlier. I am willing to learn any additional skills I need to have to do this job.

The candidate doesn't try to explain her lack of experience. Instead she talks about the skills she has (and would have given more details if she hadn't discussed them earlier) and expresses her willingness to learn new ones.

Never Say: "I don't have a lot of experience, but how can I get any if no one will hire me?" Although what she is saying is true, this answer highlights the candidate's inexperience instead of addressing her attributes and willingness to learn.

Q You've worked at the same company since you graduated from high school fifteen years ago. Why are you looking for a new job now?

A I learned a lot at my current job and I was given the opportunity to take on many different responsibilities. I decided to get some formal training to enhance my skills in bookkeeping and word processing. That training qualifies me for a job that requires greater skills than my current one does.

This candidate wants to use his new skills and therefore must change jobs. This is reasonable and shows he is motivated to do the best he can.

Never Say: "I'm bored." Many people leave their jobs because they are bored. However, that's not a good way to impress a prospective employer. The candidate should name something specific about this new job that he is looking forward to.

Q You're so young. What makes you think you can do a good job?

A I have a lot of experience in retail. I started working as a retail clerk straight out of high school, and over the last three years I worked my way up to assistant manager.

Rather than letting the interviewer lead her into a discussion about her age, this candidate leads him into a discussion about her experience.

Never Say: "What does my age have to do with it?" While it is reasonable to have reservations about the interviewer's motives, this approach is too confrontational.

Q Your resume doesn't show any formal training in this field. What do you think qualifies you for this job?

A While I don't have formal training in this field, I do have a lot of practical experience. As you can see from my resume, I spent a tremendous amount of time doing research in my last job. I plan to begin taking some courses so I can get my degree in this field.

This interviewee explains how her experience has given her the skills she needs to do this job. She also talks about her intention to get some formal training.

Never Say: "I'm going to get my degree." While this answer shows this candidate plans to develop her skills, it doesn't indicate she currently has the skills necessary for this job.

Q I see that all of your work experience has been in sales. What qualifies you to work in fundraising?

A Both sales and fundraising involve persuasion. In sales I had to persuade people to buy our products, and I was very good at it. I had the highest level of sales of anyone in my division. Now I would like to use those skills to convince people to donate money to this organization.

This candidate discusses how he can transfer his sales skills to a career in fundraising.

Never Say: "I think I will really like this field a lot more." This doesn't adequately explain why he is qualified for the job.

Q I noticed your three previous jobs were in three different cities. Why did you move around so much?

A My wife was in the Marines, but she is retired now and working as a civilian in this city, so we're finally done moving around.

As a general rule, marital status should not be discussed on a job interview. However, the candidate must explain why he has moved around so much in the past and why he won't be doing that in the future.

Never Say: "I won't be moving around a lot anymore." The interviewee should give a more elaborate answer than this one. If he doesn't want to bring up his marital status, he can say there were reasons he had to move around in the past, but some changes have brought more stability to his life.

Q I see you were manager at Wanda's Whispers. What type of business is that and what did you do there?

A Wanda's Whispers is a retail store that sells women's lingerie. I was the store manager. I interviewed, hired, and trained the store's sales team.

Although she may be embarrassed to discuss the nature of the business, she proudly discusses her responsibilities there.

Never Say: "The store sells ladies' apparel." The candidate is so flustered when she has to discuss this job that she neglects to discuss what she did there.

Q You've been out of the workforce for five years. Why re-enter it now?

A I have a lot to offer. I've developed many skills over the last five years and I want to put them to use. I have excellent organization and time management skills. I am also great at resolving conflicts.

Rather than discuss how re-entering the workforce will benefit her, this candidate instead highlights what she can bring to the job.

Never Say: "I'm in the process of getting divorced, so I have to go back to work." This is more information than the candidate should share.

Q I see you have a GED. Why did you drop out of high school?

A I guess I was young and foolish then. It was a long time ago. I thought I didn't need school anymore, but I was sadly mistaken. I got my GED three years later and then went on to college. I'm looking forward to applying my training as a registered nurse to this position.

Youthful indiscretions can be forgiven. Although this candidate dropped out of high school, he did continue his education and is planning to move forward with his career.

Never Say: "I don't remember. It was a long time ago." That isn't something one would easily forget. Since the candidate has gone on to complete his education, he shouldn't be ashamed to talk about his past.

Q You didn't start working until two years after you got your degree. What were you doing?

A I traveled extensively the year after I graduated from college. I backpacked across Europe for three months and then I spent four months in Australia. After that I traveled across the United States.

Had this candidate said that she sat at home watching television for a year after graduating, the interviewer would have assumed she was a little low on motivation. However, she explored the world, which was an admirable use of her time.

Never Say: "I needed to take some time off. College was hard." Even if this candidate didn't have as interesting a story to tell as the previous candidate, she should have explained what she did during that time.

Q You've been working outside the banking industry for the last year. Can you explain why you want to return now?

A Yes, I can. The job market, as you know, has been bad for the last year and a half. It's been impossible for someone with my qualifications to find a job in the banking industry. In order to support my family, I had to take jobs in retail sales. I was happy to see your ad for a banking job that needs someone with my skills in branch management.

This candidate's only choice is to be honest. He is not to blame for the bad job market, so he makes no excuses for working outside his field for a year.

Never Say: "I wanted to try out a new industry." It's okay to try out a new industry, but this candidate should explain why he wants to return to his old one.

Q I did a little web search and found your Facebook page. That's some very interesting stuff you posted. Care to explain?

A Everyone has a work persona and a personal time persona, I think. You should know I take my job very seriously. That means I give it my full attention while I'm working.

This job hunter forgot to make her pages private. Since the interviewer has already found potentially embarrassing material about her online, she knows it's too late for denials. All she can do at this point is stress that her private life won't interfere with her work life.

Never Say: "What page?" or "What I do on my own time is my business." Playing dumb won't work if the evidence of your after-work behavior exists online. As for the second option, while you might feel your private time is yours to do with as you wish, you need to reassure a potential employer that your behavior won't spill over into your work life by, for example, making you late to work or causing you to arrive at work with a hangover.

 Alert

Employers often search the Internet for information about prospective employees. If there's anything inappropriate about you out there in cyberspace, remove it. If you are unsure about what might be considered inappropriate, think of things you wouldn't want your grandmother to see. Make your Facebook page private if you have inappropriate content on it.

CHAPTER 14

Dealing with
Illegal Questions

Either out of ignorance or blatant disregard for antidiscrimination laws, prospective employers sometimes ask questions that are often referred to as "illegal." The employer who asks them usually doesn't have your best interests at heart. If you know what your rights are before going into an interview, you will be able to recognize inappropriate, if not illegal, questions.

Laws That Protect You from Discrimination

There are federal laws that make it illegal for employers to discriminate against employees and job applicants. These laws include Title VII of the Civil Rights Act of 1964, the Age Discrimination in Employment Act of 1967, and Title I of the Americans with Disabilities Act, all of which the Equal Employment Opportunity Commission (EEOC) oversees. The National Labor Relations Act, which is enforced by the National Labor Relations Board, is another law that protects individuals from job discrimination. The Civil Service Reform Act of 1978 prohibits federal agencies from discriminating against their workers and job applicants. Let's look at these laws in more detail to see how they can protect you.

Title VII of the Civil Rights Act of 1964

Title VII of the Civil Rights Act of 1964 prohibits employers from discriminating against employees and prospective employees because of their race, color, religion, gender, or national origin.

Race and Color Discrimination

An employer cannot reject a job candidate based on the candidate's race or color. If an interviewer requests information that will disclose the candidate's race, the EEOC interprets it to mean the information obtained will be used as a basis for making a hiring decision. The request for that information would likely be used as evidence should the candidate bring charges of discrimination against the employer.

 Alert

An employer can ask for information on race if it is needed for affirmative action purposes, in which case it would have to be kept separate from the information that is used to make a hiring decision.

National Origin Discrimination

An employer cannot discriminate against an individual because of her national origin, meaning the country she or her parents are from. Therefore, an interviewer may not ask you where you were born or where your parents were born. He may not ask you if you speak a foreign language unless it pertains to the duties of the job for which you are interviewing.

Religious Discrimination

An employer cannot use your religious beliefs to decide whether or not to hire you. An employer cannot ask you what your religion is, if you belong to any religious groups, or if you go to a house of worship. She also cannot ask if your religious beliefs prevent you from working on certain days.

Pregnancy Discrimination

The Pregnancy Discrimination Act was passed in 1978 as an Amendment to Title VII of the Civil Rights Act. It states that as long as a woman is able to perform the major functions of her job, she cannot be passed over for employment because of a pregnancy-related condition. An interviewer cannot ask if you are or plan to become pregnant.

 Fact

State and municipal laws protect against job discrimination and often take precedence over the federal laws. Some of these laws protect workers and job candidates against discrimination on the bases of sexual orientation, marital status, political affiliation, and parental status. Your local district office of the EEOC can help you determine if a prospective employer has broken a state or local law.

The Age Discrimination in Employment Act of 1967

The Age Discrimination in Employment Act makes it illegal for employers to discriminate against employees or job candidates on the basis of age. It protects those who are at least forty years old. An interviewer may not ask you how old you are, or when you graduated from high school or college, since providing that information reveals your age.

Title I of the Americans with Disabilities Act of 1990

Title I of the Americans with Disabilities Act prohibits employers from discriminating against workers or job applicants who have disabilities. This law actually makes asking some questions illegal. The ADA prohibits an employer who has not yet made a job offer from asking questions that are likely to reveal a candidate's disability. For example, an interviewer can't ask questions about health problems, such as a heart condition, asthma, or mental illness. He cannot ask a candidate if she has a disability that would keep her from performing the job. Even if a candidate has an obvious disability or reveals a hidden one, the employer cannot ask about it. There is one exception: An employer can ask a job candidate to explain how she will perform specific job functions.

An employer cannot require a candidate to take a medical exam prior to receiving a job offer. However, once the employer makes a job offer, he can make it contingent on the employee passing a medical exam, as long as the same is required of all candidates to whom the employer offers jobs in the same category. If the results of that exam reveal a disability, a job offer may be rescinded only if the employer's reason for doing so is "job-related and consistent with business necessity," according to the EEOC (U.S. Equal Employment Opportunity Commission. *ADA Enforcement Guidance: Preemployment Disability-Related Questions and Medical Examinations* on the Internet at *www.eeoc.gov/policy/docs/medfin5.pdf*).

 Question

Do antidiscrimination laws protect everyone?
Not all companies must adhere to federal discrimination laws. Only those with a certain number of employees must comply. That number varies by law but generally falls into a range of between fifteen and twenty employees.

National Labor Relations Act

The National Labor Relations Act regulates the way in which unions and private-sector employers interact. It gives employees the right to organize unions and to engage in union activities without interference from their employers. According to the National Labor Relations Board, which administers the NLRA, an employer can't discriminate against a job candidate or employee because of her union affiliation.

Civil Service Reform Act

The Civil Service Reform Act of 1978 prohibits federal agencies from discriminating against job applicants and employees on the bases of race, color, national origin, religion, sex, age, disability, marital status, political affiliation, or sexual orientation. The U.S. Office of Special Council investigates reports of discrimination against federal job applicants.

What Questions Are Illegal?

Although we often hear people talk about illegal interview questions, most discrimination laws don't prohibit any questions outright. The exception is the ADA, which actually does say it is illegal to ask a job candidate if she has a disability.

 Essential

If you believe an employer has discriminated against you, you can file a charge of discrimination with the EEOC. Call the EEOC at 1-800-669-4000 or 1-800-669-6820 (TTY) between 8:30 A.M. and 5:30 P.M. Eastern Standard Time to find out how to do this. You can also send an e-mail to *info@eeoc.gov*. In addition, instructions are available on the EEOC website, *www.eeoc.gov*.

As far as the other laws are concerned, the asking of the question itself is usually not illegal, but it is problematic; it can demonstrate the employer's intent to discriminate. If an employer uses your answer to one of these questions to deny you a job, that can be considered discriminatory.

If you envision an interviewer being carted off to the police station in handcuffs after asking you an inappropriate question, you will be disappointed to learn that is an unlikely scenario. Even if the questions were illegal or information obtained during an interview was in fact used to discriminate against you, the job candidate would have to report the employer to the EEOC before any action would be taken. The result would be a lawsuit and a possible fine, not jail time.

Questions and Answers

Q How old are you?

A I prefer to think of myself in terms of experience and not age. I have worked in this industry for quite some time. I have seen it go from a small playing field to what it is today. Fortunately, I have kept up with all the changes by taking classes and constantly updating my skills.

Rather than address the issue of age or the inappropriateness of this question, this candidate has instead decided to address some positive things about himself. He has a lot of experience and strives to keep himself abreast of changes in the industry by taking classes.

Never Say: "I'm fifty-two, but I look young for my age." This applicant should have avoided revealing his age.

Q How much do you weigh?

A My weight isn't an issue. I have never had a problem performing my job duties.

This question is not only rude, it may be illegal as well, according to the ADA. This candidate explains that her weight doesn't affect her ability to do her job.

Never Say: "I'm thinking of getting my stomach stapled." Although he has asked a rude and possibly illegal question, the employer has learned that this candidate might need some time off from work, and she hasn't even started yet.

Q What is your race?

A I'm African American and Asian.

If an employer asks a question about race, her intentions are usually not good, so make a mental note that you were asked. If the employer discriminates against you based on your race, the information you provided in this answer can be used as evidence against her if you file a complaint with the EEOC.

Never Say: "That is an illegal question. You can't ask me that." You are certainly within your rights to take an interviewer to task for asking such an inappropriate question, but the question in itself isn't illegal unless the information garnered from it is used to discriminate against you.

Q Were you born in the United States?

A I'm not sure why you're asking me that. Can you explain?

This question is inappropriate and the employer probably knows that. The candidate gives him a chance to correct himself. Perhaps the employer needs to know if the candidate is eligible to work in the United States.

Never Say: "I came here from Poland two years ago." The candidate is not required to reveal that information.

Q Where were your parents born?

A My parents came to this country thirty years ago. They worked very hard to put me through school and are very proud of my successful career. They passed their work ethic down to me.

This candidate chooses not to reveal her national origin and instead manages to talk about her own qualities. There is nothing that says a candidate shouldn't reveal her national origin, only that she doesn't have to.

Never Say: "My parents are from Greece and Portugal." This candidate is giving out more information than is necessary.

Q Your last name sounds Spanish. Is it?

A Yes, it is.

The applicant has a choice to make. He can refuse to answer or he can just give a simple answer, as he did. If this was the only question of this type, the interviewer may have just been trying to make conversation.

Never Say: "My father was born in Guatemala. My mother was born in Ireland." This candidate reveals more about his national origin than he needs to.

Q What is your sexual orientation?

A I don't think that has anything to do with this job.

Sexual orientation isn't something that should be discussed on a job interview.

Never Say: "I'm gay" or "I'm straight." While employers might, according to some state laws, be prohibited from using the answer to this question to discriminate against a job candidate because of her sexual orientation, this information isn't relevant to the job interview.

 Fact

There currently aren't any federal laws that protect private-sector employees and job applicants from discrimination based on one's sexual orientation or gender identity. Some states and local municipalities have such laws, and the Civil Service Reform Act protects federal workers from discrimination based on sexual orientation.

Q What is your religious background?

A I consider religion a very personal thing, so I would rather not discuss it.

The applicant can always choose to politely refuse to answer a question he considers improper. That is what he has decided to do.

Never Say: "How dare you ask me that?" While the candidate can refuse to answer the question, there is no reason to be that confrontational. That can certainly hurt your chances of getting hired.

Q Will your religion keep you from working on Saturday or Sunday?

A Perhaps we can discuss the details of my schedule after we both confirm that I'm the right candidate for this position.

This candidate knows Title VII of the Civil Rights Act requires that an employer reasonably accommodate the religious practices of an employee or applicant as long as doing so doesn't pose a hardship. She also knows that an employer cannot decide to reject a candidate based on the knowledge that this accommodation will be necessary. However, she chooses to wait until she receives an offer before discussing this.

Never Say: "I can't work on Saturday." Although the employer can't make a decision based on this information, it isn't necessary to discuss it at this point.

Q Do you have any children?

A I understand that you may be concerned that having a family might get in the way of someone's career. However, that has never been the case with me. I'm very dedicated to my career.

Without giving a direct answer to this question, the candidate has chosen to reassure the employer that having a family, or not having one, will not influence his career.

Never Say: "I don't have children yet." If the employer chooses not to hire this candidate, it may be because this answer indicates he might have children in the future. Whether or not this constitutes discrimination is debatable, since he doesn't currently have children.

 Essential

When faced with an improper question about your family or marital status, you can choose to address the issue head-on. You can reassure the interviewer that having a family has not and will not interfere with your career.

Q Are you planning to have children?

A I am very committed to my career. Whether or not I have children will not affect that.

This interviewee tells the employer the only thing she has the right to know—that she is dedicated to her career.

Never Say: "I've always wanted to have children." The candidate did not have to answer this question.

Q What childcare arrangements do you have in place?

A I'm sensing that you may have concerns about scheduling. I have a great attendance record on my current job. I haven't missed a day of work in two years.

This candidate has decided to address the intent of the interviewer's question. Since he believes she is afraid that child care problems will cause him to miss work, he informs her of his perfect attendance record.

Never Say: "My child goes to day care." The employer is out of line in asking this question. However, this candidate's answer only heightens her concern, since a child will not be able to go to day care when he is ill. That means Mom or Dad may have to miss work.

Q Are you married?

A No, I'm not.

Although this question is inappropriate and may even be illegal depending on state or municipal laws, the candidate sees no harm in answering it.

Never Say: "I'm getting married in six months and let's see . . . sixteen days." This answer implies that the interviewee is very immersed in her wedding plans and perhaps may not be able to give the necessary attention to her job.

Q Do you belong to a union?

A Will I be required to join a union?

The NLRA prohibits employers from questioning applicants about their union sympathies. This candidate chooses to avoid the question by asking his own.

Never Say: "Yes." The employer can't make a decision based on this information and shouldn't have asked it in the first place. The candidate certainly didn't have to answer it.

Q Are you a Democrat or Republican?

A I've always felt that it's a bad idea to discuss politics with anyone. Therefore, I'm going to refrain from answering that question.

The candidate has given a polite answer but has refused to provide the information the interviewer improperly requested.

Never Say: "I'm a Democrat." Your political affiliation has nothing to do with how well you perform on the job. There is no reason an interviewer needs to know this.

 Fact

There aren't any federal laws that protect private-sector employees or job applicants from discrimination on the basis of political affiliation. The Civil Service Reform Act prohibits federal government agencies from discriminating against employees or job candidates because of their political affiliation. Some state and local laws also make this type of discrimination illegal.

Q Will your spouse mind the long hours you will have to work here?

A I've always worked very long hours, so this won't be a problem.

This candidate chooses to address the question about the long hours she will be required to work rather than address her marital status.

Never Say: "My husband would love me to get a job with fewer hours, but there aren't many like that out there." There is no reason to give this much information. The interviewee's answer will set off some alarms. Since her husband is unhappy with her hours, she would probably take a job with fewer hours if it came along.

 Essential

When an interviewer asks you an improper question, you have three basic options. You can refuse to answer it, you can confront the interviewer, or you can answer it. Information you give voluntarily can be used against the employer if he discriminates.

Q How do you want to be addressed? Miss or Mrs.?

A You can just call me Robin.

The interviewer is trying to ascertain the candidate's marital status, but she won't play into it. She dodges the issue altogether.

Never Say: "I prefer Mrs. Brown." The candidate could have avoided letting the interviewer know her marital status.

Q Have you ever been arrested or convicted of a crime?

A No. I have never been convicted of a crime.

According to the law in many states, an employer may not ask you if you have ever been arrested, but, depending on where the employer is located, he may be able to ask you if you've been convicted of a crime. In some states, convictions for certain types of crimes can be taken into account when considering whether to hire a job candidate. Notice how this candidate avoids the arrest question. She doesn't want to lie or discuss an arrest that she was not convicted for.

Never Say: "I was arrested once but I wasn't convicted." Again, depending on the law in your state, the employer may only ask about prior convictions. The applicant may not have to talk about her arrest at all.

Q Have you ever committed a crime?

A If you're asking if I've ever been convicted of a crime, no I haven't been.

If the employer is located in a state that prohibits discrimination based on a candidate's arrest record, but allows hiring decisions to be made based on whether or not someone has been convicted, the applicant is not required to reveal prior arrests or criminal behavior.

Never Say: "Yes, but I was never convicted."

Q I see you're limping. Did you hurt yourself?

A I'm fine, thank you.

The employer, according to the ADA, cannot inquire about an applicant's injury and the candidate is under no obligation to reveal it.

Never Say: "I have cerebral palsy." The candidate is not required to reveal any information regarding his disability.

 Question

What should I do if I was in jail?
If you were convicted of a felony, it will be revealed in a background check. You might as well be up front about it. If the prospective employer is located in a state that only allows a conviction to weigh into a hiring decision if it's for a crime directly related to the job, the law might protect you from discrimination.

Q Do you have a heart condition?

A With all due respect, I don't have to answer that question.

The applicant has a right to refuse to answer this question. The ADA makes it illegal for an employer to ask questions about a job candidate's health.

Never Say: "Yes, I do." The employer is legally prohibited from asking this question and the candidate does not have to answer it.

 Fact

The ADA prohibits an employer from asking about the nature of an applicant's disability. It does allow an employer to inquire about a candidate's ability to perform a job-related task and, in some cases, may even ask the applicant to demonstrate how she will perform that task.

Q Will you need us to make any accommodations in order for you to do your job?

A I am able to perform all functions of the job as you described it.

The ADA prohibits the employer from asking this question, even if he asks it of all applicants.

Never Say: "Yes, I will." The applicant doesn't have to answer this question. If she chooses to, the employer can't decide not to hire her because of her answer, unless the accommodations she needs will cause the employer undue hardship.

Q Have you ever been treated for mental health problems?

A I have, but everything is under control now. I have always performed well at work and I know I will continue to.

Although he is under no obligation to reveal this information at any time, this candidate doesn't want to lie to his employer and knows that the truth may come out at some point in the future.

Never Say: "No, I haven't" if you have. This candidate just lied to his prospective employer. Although he is within his legal rights to withhold information regarding his mental health, he has to consider whether he plans to reveal this information at a later date and what the consequences may be if he does. Although the employer can't fire an employee because of the employee's mental illness, she may distrust him for lying, which will damage their relationship. He would be better off telling the truth or simply saying he'd rather not discuss it.

Q Have you ever been treated for drug addiction?

A That was some time ago, and I prefer not to discuss it.

This candidate is within his rights not to discuss this. Those who have been treated for drug addiction are covered by the ADA, and a hiring decision cannot be based upon this.

Never Say: "Yes, and I've only slipped up twice since then." The ADA doesn't protect someone who is currently using drugs from discrimination.

Q Do you currently take any prescription drugs?

A I've taken medication from time to time, but it has never affected my work.

The candidate doesn't have to answer this question but doesn't want to be dishonest. It's her call to make. This answer does not reveal whether the candidate is currently taking medication, and by law she doesn't have to reveal that.

Never Say: "Yes, I take pain medication." There is no reason the candidate needed to reveal such specific information.

 Fact

An employer can refuse to hire someone who currently uses illegal drugs. The ADA does not protect the applicant in this case. In addition, tests for illegal drugs are not subject to the ADA's restrictions on medical examinations.

Q Whom should we notify in case of an emergency?

A I have to give it some thought. Can I let you know?

The employer does not need this information before the employee begins to work for her. This may be a thinly disguised attempt to learn about the candidate's personal life; for example, his marital status.

Never Say: "You can notify my wife. Her name is . . ." This answer reveals more than the employer needs to know about the candidate's personal life.

Q Asked of a candidate applying for a job with the U.S. government: "Are you gay?"

A That isn't relevant to this job.

While a job candidate may or may not choose to answer this question, her answer can't play a role in a federal government agency's decision to hire her. The Civil Service Reform Act protects federal job applicants from discrimination.

Never Say: "None of your business." Being confrontational is never the right way to go, even if you feel a question is inappropriate, rude, or even illegal. If you don't want to share this information, it is always best to be polite.

Q Do you want to have dinner on Saturday night? We can discuss your job qualifications over a nice bottle of pinot.

A I'll have to say no thank you. I never mix business with pleasure.

If the interviewer is persistent or in any way makes the candidate feel like he will get a job offer only by going out on a date with her, this may be considered sexual harassment, which is illegal under Title VII of the Civil Rights Act of 1964 and can be reported to the EEOC. The candidate makes it clear that the employer's advances are unwelcome, a necessary element to a sexual harassment claim.

Never Say: "What time on Saturday?" The job candidate should never acquiesce to this kind of advance.

CHAPTER 15

Behavioral Interviews

B ehavioral interviews take the concept of using real-life examples to demonstrate your attributes a few steps further than discussed earlier in this book. You will not only have the opportunity to talk about when you used a particular attribute, but also explain how you used it.

Behavioral Interviews: The Basics

Potential employers use behavioral interviews to help determine how job candidates will react to certain situations based on how they responded to similar experiences in the past.

How Behavioral Interview Techniques Help Employers

When an employer conducts an interview, his main objective is to make sure the person he hires can do the job. The best way to find this out is to actually watch him do it. Generally, though, a prospective employer has to assess several candidates for an open position and time is usually of the essence when it comes to making a decision. In most cases it would be inefficient to evaluate job candidates by actually observing them. Furthermore, since many people are currently employed while they are engaged in a job search, it would be difficult to schedule these "auditions."

In lieu of actually trying out job candidates, what can an employer do? Many employers use a technique called *behavioral interviewing*, which relies on the theory that past behavior is a good predictor of future behavior. Specifically, this type of interview attempts to determine how the job candidate drew upon her competencies to handle situations in a previous job or jobs in order to predict how she will handle similar situations if this employer hires her.

What Happens During a Behavioral Interview?

Before an employer begins interviewing candidates, he will determine what knowledge, skills, and abilities are required for the job. Together these are referred to as "competencies," which may include the following:

- Decision-making skills
- Time-management skills
- Problem-solving skills
- Organizational skills
- The ability to multitask
- Interpersonal skills
- Writing and presentation skills
- The ability to work on and build teams
- Flexibility

Then the interviewer will ask you to demonstrate that you have these competencies. You will have to draw upon real-life examples that illustrate how you used a particular competency in a work-related situation.

How to Answer Behavioral Questions

When answering behavioral questions, you want to show the interviewer you have a particular competency, and you've used it to benefit a past employer. Behavioral questions require possibly the most preparation of any asked on a job interview.

Find out what competencies an employer requires. You may find them listed in the job description; if not, dig deeper.

Once you know what competencies the employer requires, come up with anecdotes highlighting them. Look to your work history, or school experiences, to find situations in which you used your knowledge, skills, and abilities to successfully solve a problem or complete a project.

When she asks a question, the interviewer probably won't state what competency she expects you to demonstrate in your answer. You have to quickly analyze the question to figure it out. Begin your answer by presenting the task or problem you faced. Then explain the steps you took to accomplish or solve it, highlighting the competencies you used. Give as many details as necessary to demonstrate each competency she is looking for, but be careful not to go off on a tangent.

Questions and Answers

Q Tell me about something you've done to motivate your coworkers.

A About a year ago, our company went through some tough times and about twenty-five workers were laid off. Morale was lower than I had ever seen it. This happened right around the time we had to start putting together our holiday issue, and no one was really into it. I planned a "winter in July" party to pick up everyone's spirits and to get us ready to work on the magazine. By the time the party was over, we were all in a better mood and we were ready to put together a great issue. I think it was one of the best ones we ever did.

The job candidate has demonstrated that he knows how to motivate others.

Q What is the toughest group you had to get to cooperate with you?

A I was asked to teach a new procedure to the customer service team. I had heard rumblings to the effect that many people on the team were unhappy with the new procedure, so I knew I wasn't going to have a receptive group to work with. Before I could be effective at teaching them what they needed to know, I had to convince them that the new procedure would benefit them. I set up a presentation that explained how it would save them time. Once the team saw the benefits of the new procedure, they actually looked forward to the training. They learned very quickly and were able to implement the procedure in less than a week.

The interviewee demonstrates two competencies in her response. She highlights her interpersonal skills when she talks about how she was aware of the customer service team's concerns. Then she highlights her presentation skills.

Q Describe a situation in which you had a positive influence on someone else's actions.

A One of the new guys in my department was assigned a couple of projects at once and couldn't figure out how he would get both of them done on time. He was really frantic, since he had only been there for a short time and was approaching his first performance evaluation. He knew only too well that these projects were crucial to his getting a good evaluation. When he told me about his concerns, I asked him how he was scheduling his work and whether he was setting deadlines for completing different portions of his project. He had no idea what I was talking about. This was his first real job, and it required a different sort of time management than his college courses had. I spent a lunch hour teaching him how to set up work schedules. After we met, he set up work schedules for both projects and asked me to look them over. I did and helped him make a couple of changes. He completed both projects by their deadlines and got a pretty good performance evaluation.

In describing how she helped her colleague, this candidate shows that she has good interpersonal skills. She also manages to demonstrate her own time-management skills by describing how she taught her coworker to set a schedule for himself.

 Fact

> In today's workplace, most people work on teams. A team must function as a single entity whose goal it is to complete a project efficiently and effectively. Members of teams must appreciate one another's differences and be willing to compromise. You must be able to demonstrate that you can work well as part of a team.

Q We expect the person we hire for this job to be able to take charge of a couple of big projects. Are you ready for that?

A A few months ago, the chairperson of my department asked me to assemble a committee, made up of faculty and students, to evaluate the current curriculum. He gave us two semesters to complete the project. The first thing I had to do was decide whom to include on the committee. I chose a few members of the faculty who had been with us for a very long time, as well as some who had recently joined the department. The students I picked ranged from freshmen to graduate students. I wanted a wide cross-section of both faculty and students. After that I set up deadlines for certain parts of the project to be completed, and I set up a schedule for meetings. Finally, each person was assigned a specific area to look at and then present for discussion at each meeting. Based on the work of this committee, we were able to drop some courses that were not effectively meeting the goals of the department, and we were able to add innovative courses that would attract students.

By giving this answer, the candidate demonstrates that she is good at organizing and planning projects.

Q Have you ever been a member of a group where some of the members did not work well together? Describe what you did.

A Yes, I have. I was a member of a group that was developing a new software program for kids. There were three of us on the team. I got along with the two people I was working with, but they didn't get along with each other at all. They constantly shot down each other's ideas and expected me to take sides. I refused to do that. Instead I tried to help them see each other's point of view. I explained how they each had good ideas and helped them compromise. In the end, we had a very successful product.

With this answer, the job candidate demonstrates that he has good interpersonal skills and good team-building skills.

 Question

What should I do if I can't use a real-life experience to demonstrate a competency?
If you can't draw upon real-life experience to answer a question, don't make something up. You can use a hypothetical situation as an example, but let the interviewer know you are doing that.

Q Give an example of a time when you went above and beyond the call of duty.

A I've been teaching algebra for seven years, and I know some children really have difficulty understanding it. There's only so much individual attention I can give to each student during class, so any help I give them has to be at another time. I teach five classes a day, which leaves only two free periods. One is a prep period and one is my lunchtime. I decided the kids needed math help more than I needed lunch, so I set aside three times a week when they could come to my room for tutoring. Many students have taken me up on this extra help and their grades have improved significantly.

Most of my students do really well on the statewide seventh-grade test as a result of my tutoring them.

This candidate demonstrates how she solved a problem within the time constraints of her job. She shows how her students and the school benefited.

Q Have you ever been assigned several projects at the same time? How did you handle it?

A That happens very often, but one time that stands out in my mind is last year during the fall. The managers of three departments—women's outerwear, toys, and women's accessories—asked me to set up their winter holiday displays. They all wanted them up within a week. I knew there was no way I could complete all three in one week. Since I know customers are more likely to shop for kids' presents first and kids really enjoy the displays, I decided to decorate the toy department first. I checked with the other two managers to see if they had some flexibility in their scheduling, and both did. So I scheduled both departments to have their displays up the following week. All three departments were beautifully decorated for the holidays, and I completed them all in two weeks.

This interviewee demonstrates knowledge about his industry when he discusses why he chose to decorate the toy department first. He goes on to show how he is good at planning and scheduling.

Q Can you give an example of how you adjust to unforeseen circumstances?

A Last summer I was less than a week away from a big presentation. I was in the middle of preparing for it when all of a sudden, the power went out. We soon found out the lights were out everywhere on the East Coast and there were no estimates of how long that would be the case. Fortunately, I was two days ahead of schedule in my preparation, but since I didn't know when power would be restored, I was worried I wouldn't be able to work on it. I knew if I wasn't ready on time, my company would look bad and it could cost us a lot of money. Our battery backup was still working, so I decided to print out the presentation. I wrote a lot of the presentation by hand that day. All I had left to do were my slides, which I did when the power came back on the next afternoon.

The job candidate shows that he knows how to cope with an emergency.

Q Give an example of a quick decision you made.

A When we were working on our April issue last year, one of the designers we planned to feature backed out just before the photo shoot because she didn't feel her line was ready. We had planned to feature her work on about twenty pages. Now we had to figure out what to do with those pages. We didn't have much time to waste. The photographer was on his way and was going to get paid for a day's work whether we used him or not. It turned out one of my assistant editors knew an up-and-coming designer. I decided to take a chance on the new designer, since I trusted my assistant's opinion. The shoot was wonderful and her designs were fantastic. The issue was great and we've featured that designer a few times since then.

This interviewee shows that she knows how to make quick decisions.

Q This is a busy office and we have a lot of projects going on at once. Everyone who works here must be able to multitask. Can you?

A Since I work for three lawyers, I regularly have to multitask. Just two weeks ago they walked into my office one after another, handed me files, and told me they needed the work in them completed by the end of the week. I looked at the files and I figured out how long each assignment would take. Then I looked to see if there was any overlap between the assignments. I discovered that each required some research, which I was able to do that afternoon. The next morning I began working on the first project. I needed some additional files to do the other two projects, so I asked one of the file clerks to retrieve those for me while I put the finishing touches on the first assignment. With those files in front of me, I was able to work on the other two assignments.

While explaining his ability to multitask, this candidate also highlights his project-planning skills and his ability to delegate some work to others.

Q Give me an example of when you showed initiative and took the lead on a project.

A A year ago, we noticed that our students' grades on statewide language arts exams were slipping. I had recently attended a seminar that addressed this particular issue and ways to resolve it. I had a program in mind that I thought we could implement at our school. I spoke to my principal about it, and she asked me to write a formal proposal. After I did that and she approved it, I put together a committee of teachers and parents who would work with me to implement the program. This year's exam, as you know, won't take place until next month, but I think we'll see big improvements.

By giving this answer, the candidate shows how he recognized a problem and took initiative in resolving it.

Q Tell me about a report you had to write.

A My boss asked me to develop a plan to improve our quality-control process. She gave me a month to come up with three different ideas and said she would choose the best one based on my report. The first thing I noticed was that we didn't have a written document that described the procedure we were currently using, so I had to put one together. Then I began to research quality-control processes used by other companies. The librarian at our local library was able to tell me what databases I could access to find articles that discussed this issue. Through my research, I was able to find which quality-control processes were most successful. I chose the three that I thought would work best for my employer and wrote about them. The report included my recommendation as to which one I thought we should use. My boss was pleased with the report. She agreed with my recommendation, and my next project involved implementing the new process, including writing a document that described it completely.

This answer demonstrates this candidate's ability to put together a written report, including using research skills.

 Essential

Certain soft skills are vital to one's performance at work. Without these skills, the employee simply can't do his job. Make a point of demonstrating that you have these valuable skills, even if you aren't specifically asked about them. They include multitasking, organizing, time management, and decision making.

Q Give me an example of how you dealt with a conflict between two of your employees.

A A year ago, two of my employees started having problems getting along with each other. It came from out of the blue but looked like it had the potential to escalate rapidly. I called separate meetings with each of the employees. They had remarkably similar stories and didn't blame each other for their hard feelings. They agreed on a joint meeting, where I was able to help them realize that they really were on the same page after all. Things between them are now back to the way they were. They are both productive members of my department, so I'm glad we were able to work things out.

This candidate demonstrates her skill in conflict resolution.

Q Describe a recent unpopular decision you made and what the result was.

A A few months ago, we found that we were having difficulty scheduling people to cover the circulation desk during lunch hours. Almost everyone wanted to go to lunch at 1 P.M., which meant we wouldn't have enough people around to check books in and out for our patrons. I decided that the only way to deal with this was to schedule lunch hours. We had two lunch hours—noon to 1 P.M. and 1 P.M. to 2 P.M. Staff could go to lunch only at the time they were assigned. No one liked this idea very much because they were used to going to lunch whenever they felt like it. Something had to be done, however, because if we didn't do something, service would suffer. Scheduled lunch hours have been in effect for the past three months. The staff has gotten used to it and service has definitely improved.

The interviewer shows he is a good manager who isn't afraid to make decisions that may be unpopular.

Q Have you ever had to work with someone with whom you had a bad relationship? How did you handle it?

A My boss asked me to work on a project with the one person in my company I don't get along with. I knew we'd be working together for several months, and I didn't want those months to be miserable. I decided to swallow my pride and invite my coworker to lunch. We discussed the project and what we would have to do to make it work. We both realized that the company would be the victim if we let our personal differences get in the way of our performance. We divided the project up so that we could each work independently using our individual strengths, but we wound up working together more than we expected, so we learned to appreciate each other's strengths and how to use them in combination to benefit the company. We completed the project, and we've worked on several other ones together since then by choice. Even though we still don't always agree on things, we know how to work well together now.

The candidate demonstrates how she used her interpersonal skills to resolve her differences with her coworker.

 Fact

> When an employer hires someone, he is investing in that person's future at his company. The more successful that person is and the longer she stays, the bigger the return on the investment. If he makes a poor hiring decision, that investment won't pay off because the person won't succeed and won't stick around. That is one reason employers take job interviewing very seriously.

Q Tell me about a recent situation in which you had to deal with a very upset customer.

A Just last week, one of our customers called and was extremely upset because something we had shipped to him arrived damaged. One of his customers was coming in to pick up the item two days later, and he didn't want to disappoint her. I assured him that he would have the item for his customer on time. I brought the merchandise to the shipping department myself and asked that it be sent out by overnight delivery. He called the next day to say his package had arrived. He thanked us for resolving this quickly and placed another order.

The candidate has demonstrated how his good interpersonal skills kept a customer happy and resulted in another sale.

Q Tell me about the most difficult person you've ever had to work with.

A That would have to be Jen. Jen was a perfectly nice person, but she liked giving her work to others. She didn't have the right to do that. Our supervisor was the one who assigned work to us, and he expected each of us to handle that work on our own. One day I decided I had had enough of this. Jen asked me to make some phone calls for her, and I told her we needed to have a talk. We did, and it turned out that Jen was overwhelmed by all the work our boss assigned and didn't know how to handle it, other than by getting help from her coworkers. I helped her figure out a way to manage her time better and get her work done on her own. Jen is doing a lot better now. She doesn't try to pass off her work to other people anymore.

This candidate shows he has good interpersonal skills and is willing to help others succeed.

Q Describe a situation in which you were able to effectively "read" another person and guide your actions based on what you understood about her needs and values.

A About eight months ago, a client approached us about a new product they were introducing. There were two people I could have assigned to work on that project. Both would have done a good job; they are equally skilled and had worked with the client before. Knowing what I know about one of those employees, I had a feeling this new product was contrary to some of his personal values. I didn't want to jump to any conclusions, so I spoke to him before I made a decision about this. I was correct. He would have worked on the project, but he wouldn't have been comfortable with it. I decided to assign it to the other person. The client was very happy with the way things went. The product was introduced over the summer and has been very successful. They've had sales of about $1.5 million.

This candidate demonstrates her interpersonal skills by giving this answer.

Q Have you ever anticipated a problem while working on a project and found a way to avoid it?

A While working on a project in October, I realized the person who had done the budget hadn't included printing costs. It wasn't going to be a huge expense, but it was definitely something that needed to be included in the budget. First I figured out what the cost of printing would be. Then I looked at the rest of the budget to see if the other costs on it were accurate, and I found a few places where the costs had been overstated a little bit. I was able to change some numbers around so the money allotted for those expenses could instead be used for printing. We were still a little short, so I had to talk to my boss about increasing the budget. He was able to do that because the amount we needed wasn't very significant.

Not only does this candidate demonstrate that she can antici-pate and avoid problems, she also shows that she knows how to budget expenses.

 Alert

Your goals should always be aligned with those of the employer. If the employer senses that your goals have nothing to do with your pro-spective job, you probably won't be working for him anytime soon. Goals like cutting costs and increasing productivity are always appre-ciated. Reaching your own goals will be a by-product of that.

Q Have you ever found working on a team disappoint-ing? Did you do anything that helped things improve?

A In a business course I took in college, we were assigned to teams to work on a project that involved running a mock company. At the beginning we had trouble working together. However, we were being graded as a group, so we had to find a way to utilize our differences rather than let them defeat us. I thought the project would be more successful if we drew on every member's strengths and interests. Once I explained this to everyone, we again divided up the tasks, using our different strengths and interests to put together a successful project. We ended up earning an A.

The interviewee takes this opportunity to demonstrate her team-building skills as well as her leadership skills.

Q Tell me about a problem you solved.

A I was coordinating a trade show in Washington, D.C. We advertised in all the industry publications and got an unprecedented number of responses from vendors who wanted to display their products. There were 350 companies that wanted to reserve booths. I knew our current venue had insufficient space. We could have turned away some of the vendors, but since they represented a significant amount of revenue, I didn't think this was even an option. I started looking into larger venues. I thought the Washington Convention Center would be perfect. There was plenty of room to accommodate everyone, and with the extra participation we were able to afford the larger site. We went ahead and booked it. The trade show was very successful. Both attendees and vendors were thrilled with the event. Many expressed an interest in attending next year.

The interviewee demonstrates his problem-solving skills.

Q Tell me about a time when you had to use your presentation skills to influence a client.

A My former employer had one particular client who had to be convinced that our way was the best way to go every time we made a presentation. She always needed a lot of reassurance, which was her right, since she was paying good money for our services. There was one particular project I worked on for her where she needed even more convincing than usual. She wanted to redesign the packaging for one of her hair-care products. We put together a package design that was unique; the bottle was oval shaped instead of the usual cylindrical shape. It would really stand out from everything else on the shelves. Since it was an unconventional design and she was pretty conservative, she was hesitant to proceed. I asked our research department to put together some focus groups. Ninety percent of those we surveyed said they liked the new design better than the old one, and 85 percent picked that product from a group of three other similar products. We presented that information to the client and sold her on the oval shape. She went ahead with it and saw a 22 percent increase in sales in the first six months after the new design was introduced.

This interviewee demonstrates his presentation skills as he is asked to and shows how he was able to influence his client's decision.

 Fact

Always use actual figures to prove your point. If you are talking about increasing sales, raising money, or cutting costs, for example, give the actual dollar amount or the percentage of increase or decrease. For example, say that you increased sales by 20 percent or cut costs by $300,000.

Q Tell me how you delegate work effectively.

A One of our clients asked us to work on a major project for them. It involved a conference they were holding in six months. They expected thousands of people to attend and they needed us to help them choose a location, get the best rates on hotels, find caterers, and then organize the event. I picked three people on my staff to work on this project with me. One person had a lot of experience in travel, so I asked her to choose the location and work with some hotels in the area to get us the best rates for those who were attending the conference. Another person had worked on an event for a different client and had done a great job choosing the caterer, so I asked him to arrange for the meals and refreshments. Finally, I picked the most organized person on my staff to collect responses from those who had signed up for the conference. She had to assign them to tables for meals and had to figure out who would attend which conference events. I have to say my staff did a great job. I was so proud of them. More than 5,000 people attended the conference and all went well.

This candidate shows how he was able to delegate work to those who were most suitable for each assignment.

Q Give me an example of a time when you used your fact-finding skills to solve a problem.

A I was advisor to a student who needed to request a leave of absence from the university. I didn't know what the proper procedures were to officially do this. I didn't want to have her do it incorrectly and then be inadvertently dropped from the program. I asked our department secretary if there was a written document that discussed the procedure. He didn't know of one, so I contacted the registrar's office. They referred me to the associate dean's office. I finally got the answer there and was able to tell the student what she needed to do.

The candidate, as asked, demonstrates how she used her fact-finding skills.

 Question

Is it okay to make it seem as if I have experience I don't really have?
Never lie on a job interview. While having insufficient experience lowers your chances of getting hired, getting caught in a lie pretty much guarantees that you won't get the job. Instead of lying, talk about your related experience and explain how it is similar to what your prospective employer wants.

Q Tell me about a time when you had to make an unpopular decision.

A As director of our after-school program, I noticed that parents were often arriving very late to pick up their children. That meant that staff had to stay late too, which meant we had to pay them for their time. We simply didn't have the money to do that. I decided we would have to charge parents if they were late in order to have the money to pay our staff. Many people weren't happy with this, but we really didn't have a choice. This was enough incentive to get most parents to pick up their children on time. As a matter of fact, late pickups decreased by 85 percent right after this program went into effect.

This answer demonstrates that the candidate is willing to make an unpopular decision in order to solve a problem.

Q Tell me about a project you initiated.

A Last February, my boss took a three-week vacation. He left me some work to do while he was gone, but I finished it by the end of the first week. I had wanted to reorganize our files for a long time, and now I had the time to work on this. First I developed a plan to work on the project. I set up a schedule that included setting goals for what I wanted to complete by the end of each day in order to finish within two weeks. Then I figured out what filing system I wanted to use. I recruited our intern to help me. We finished the project on the Friday before my boss was set to return. He was happy to see what I had done while he was gone.

This answer demonstrates several competencies. The candidate takes initiative when she takes on a project without being asked. She shows that she knows how to plan and schedule a project and also how to delegate tasks.

Q Describe a big presentation you had to deliver.

A I had to make a big presentation at a national trade show. I was standing in for my supervisor, who had to be somewhere else that day. He gave me the assignment two weeks before the show, so I had to prepare the presentation within a pretty tight time frame. First I set goals for completing each part of the presentation. Then I scheduled meetings with the developers of the products I'd have to present at the show so I could make sure I knew everything I could about them. I put together a great presentation. We took orders from 150 retailers that day alone, and the sales on the products I presented increased by 15 percent after the show.

The candidate highlights her time-management skills when she describes how she put together a presentation within a tight time frame. She also highlights her presentation skills. Notice that she backs up her answers by using real numbers.

 Essential

When deciding which accomplishments to discuss on a job interview, you should always select those that best demonstrate your ability to do the job for which you are interviewing. For example, if you are interviewing for a job in an accounting firm and you've previously worked at one, use examples from that experience rather than from your experience at an advertising agency.

Q How have you convinced your boss that your approach is the best one to take in order to complete a project?

A Before I started working for my current employer, employees rarely worked in teams. I knew of many projects that a team could handle more effectively than an individual could, but I couldn't seem to convince anyone else. Then my boss's supervisor asked him to work on a huge project with a very tight deadline. Even though my supervisor is a talented man, this project clearly needed the talents of many different people to be successful. But I had to make him see that. I put together a list of people in different departments who had the necessary skills to help complete the project. I presented this list to my boss and sold him on the idea of putting together a team. He and his new team completed the project and his boss was extremely happy with it. My supervisor often uses teams to complete projects now.

This job candidate demonstrates how she was able to persuade her boss that her approach was the best one to take and goes as far as discussing the outcome of the project.

Q What you do when you have a conflict with a client?

A Last March I was working on a client's project that required us to hire a researcher. We worked closely with the client to draw up a contract with the researcher, who then completed the work. The client then decided he wanted some additional research done, but didn't want to pay for it. Of course, our researcher couldn't work for free, so we worked out a deal with her. We "loaned" her one of our interns to assist her, and she was able to charge less for the work she did. The client was happy that he got what he wanted and didn't have to pay full price for it. We were happy because he was pleased with our work, which meant that he would probably return in the future.

This interviewee shows how he resolved a conflict with a client by coming up with a solution with which everyone was happy.

CHAPTER 16

Do You Have Any Questions?

If you like talking about yourself, you'll get your fill when you go on job interviews. Each one will revolve around you. The interviewer will spend time asking questions to learn as much about you as possible, and use your answers to determine whether to hire you. When you've told her all she wants to know, the interviewer will offer you the chance to ask questions, learning almost as much from your questions as from your answers to her inquiries.

Asking Questions Is a Must

Never forgo the chance to ask a prospective employer questions. Perhaps the most important reason for asking questions at the conclusion of a job interview is that it helps you learn about the employer. The information you gather, in addition to the research you did before the interview, can help you decide whether you will want to consider a job offer from this employer. Let's say, though, you think you already know enough about this particular company to make a decision. You did a lot of research prior to the interview and, based on what you know, you'd accept a decent job offer. What would be the point of asking questions if you already have all the information you need? There are reasons for asking questions at the conclusion of a job interview that go beyond helping you decide whether you want to work for the company.

When you ask questions, you indicate to the interviewer you are interested in the job. Since the company will probably want to avoid making an offer to a candidate who will reject it, not asking questions may take you out of the running for the job because it will make you look disinterested.

Your questions can either demonstrate to the interviewer that you were paying attention during the interview, or they can show her you were not. Questions that follow up on points that were discussed during the interview are good. For example, if you need clarification on something, this would be a good time to ask for it. However, if you ask simple questions that she already answered at some point during the interview, you will seem as if you drifted off. When you are working from a list of questions you prepared in advance, remember to eliminate those that were already answered.

 Essential

Make a mental note of questions that pop into your head during the interview. You may even come up with questions based on the ones the interviewer asks you. To show you were listening, preface questions that are related to something that was said during the interview with "You mentioned that . . ." or "When you said that . . ."

If you phrase them the right way, your questions can give the interviewer a chance to picture you as her new hire. Instead of asking "What role will the person you hire play in the company's plans for expansion," ask "What role will I play in the company's plans for expansion?" This not only demonstrates your interest in the job, it also encourages the interviewer to consider your qualifications for the job and how you fit into the company's future plans.

Finally, asking questions can show off some of your attributes. A job candidate who asks intelligent questions demonstrates he is a careful decision maker who needs to gather information before making a life-changing decision, such as accepting a job offer. Your questions can also serve as proof that you are a motivated person who came to the interview fully prepared. Ask questions that are based on research you did prior to the interview.

Preparing Your Questions

You should prepare a list of questions in advance, and make them specific to each organization with which you are interviewing. First, consider the information you will need in order to decide if you want to work for this company. Among the things you might want to know are its future plans for growth, its current financial health, rates of employee turnover, and levels of job satisfaction among employees. You probably will also want to know what your opportunities for advancement might be.

You are likely to come up with more questions during the interview. As mentioned previously, don't be afraid to ask for clarification of anything you didn't understand. Questions about salary, benefits, and vacation time are off limits at this point. Hold on to those until the employer makes an official job offer.

Questions You *Should* Ask and Questions You *Should Not* Ask

Q Where would I be working?

This question is a practical one. Pity the person who accepts a job offer only to find out he has to relocate. From your research, you will have learned whether the employer has offices elsewhere. A job advertisement will generally indicate which office has the job opening; if not, this is a fine question to ask.

Q Is there a written job description? May I see it?

You will ask this question simply because you need this information to make an informed decision about whether or not to accept the job.

Q How long have you worked here?

The person interviewing you has a position that is probably sev-eral steps above the one for which you are interviewing. Given that fact, the answer to this question will indicate how long it typically takes employees to advance within the company. If the owner of the company is interviewing you, there is no reason to ask this question.

Q What do you like most about your job with this company?

The interviewer is likely one of the few employees of the com-pany with whom you will have contact before you are hired. See what she has to say about working there. The answer to this ques-tion, if the interviewer is honest, will weigh into your decision about accepting a job offer. As with the previous question, ask this only of employees and not the owner of the company.

Q In your opinion, what is the best part of this job?

Along the same lines, the answer you receive may help you decide whether the job is right for you. It can also provide you with some valuable insight into the job, especially if your interviewer held the job before being promoted.

Q What is the chain of command?

When you ask questions about the inner workings of a com-pany, it indicates to the employer that you are interested in the job.

Q Who will I be reporting to?

If you find out who your immediate supervisor is, you can try to learn about that person after the interview. Don't forget that you should be gathering information that will help you decide whether to accept an offer if one is made.

Q How many others are in my department?

This will give you a feel for how many people you will work with on a daily basis and what the structure of the group is like. Once again, your prospective employer will be able to note your interest in the position.

Q Please describe the corporate culture in this office.

You'll be able to gauge whether this is an environment in which you can see yourself working and being happy.

Q How much interoffice interaction is there? Do departments tend to work independently of one another, or is there a fair amount of intercommunication?

The interviewer will be able to tell you who you'll be working with most often, and if your duties may require you to gain some understanding of other groups within the company.

 Essential

When it comes to asking questions, you should always have some prepared for the interviewer ahead of time. While you may want to write these down for your own reference before the interview, never read directly from this list during the interview.

Q What will I need to do to advance?

Asking this question shows you will be a productive employee who is interested in doing the best job possible. You will do what you need to do to move up.

Q What are my chances for advancement here?

Similar in nature to the previous question, this question shows the employer you are motivated. It also allows you to find out if you will have the opportunity to advance should you work for this employer. That information will help you decide whether to accept a job offer, since you don't want to languish in the same position for a long time.

Q How many people have held this position in the last three years? Why did they leave?

If there is a high rate of turnover in the position for which you are interviewing, you should be suspicious. You should try to find out why this is the case. Is this a difficult employer to work for? Or perhaps the company has expectations that are impossible for employees to meet and they are fired for not meeting them. If you haven't already, access your network to find out if anyone has had any experience with this employer.

Q How long do most employees stay?

Learning about turnover is a good way to gauge whether employees enjoy working for the employer. A high rate of turnover indicates that most employees aren't satisfied with their jobs, while a low rate of turnover demonstrates a high level of job satisfaction.

Q What reason do most employees give for leaving?

The answer to this question expands on the answer to the prior question. Knowing why employees leave the company helps you find out what you may or may not like about working there. Of course, the interviewer may not know the answer to this question or may not be willing to share it.

Q How will you decide whom to hire?

The answer to this question will let you find out if you missed something during the interview. Was there another skill or qualification the employer is seeking that you didn't get to talk about? If there was one, try to briefly mention it. If the interviewer seems to be rushing you out the door, it may have to wait. You can use your thank-you letter to talk about something that was missed during the interview.

Q When will I hear from you about a decision?

If you know when the employer will make a hiring decision, you won't be left in a state of limbo waiting for the phone to ring. If you don't hear from the employer by a day or two after she says a decision will be made, you can call her. Finally, if you are continuing to interview for other jobs, which you should do until you receive and accept a job offer, you might want to schedule future interviews after the decision date if it's coming up soon.

 Question

What does it mean when an interviewer avoids answering certain questions?
If the interviewer avoids answering reasonable questions—for example, ones about employee turnover—it should send up some red flags for you. What he doesn't say speaks much louder than what he does say. Try to learn more before accepting an offer

Q What is the next step? Are you doing second interviews?

This will simply help you know what to expect next.

Q How often are performance evaluations conducted and how are the evaluations made?

You will ask this question to learn what working for this company will be like. You may get a sense of how strict the managers are or how closely the staff is monitored. If you are interviewing for a management position, you will get a sense of how much of your time you will spend on evaluation paperwork.

Q You mentioned something about a training period. How long is it?

This question indicates your interest in the job and shows that you were listening during the interview.

Q Will I have any other opportunities for training?

An employee who inquires about training opportunities is willing to learn as much as possible to do a good job.

Q What types of assignments will I have?

This question indicates you are interested in the job. It also allows you to learn what you will be doing if you are hired.

Alert

Phrase questions in the first, rather than third, person. For example, ask "When will I . . ." rather than "When will the person you hire . . ." Doing this will show you are confident and will allow the employer to picture you on the job.

Q How has the company grown over the last five years? Is it profitable?

A company's financial health will help you decide whether to accept a job offer. If the company hasn't grown over the last five years or if it isn't profitable, this may signal that it might not be in the best financial health. Should you accept a job offer, you may be looking for work again soon.

Q What does the company plan to do to keep growing, and what role would I play?

The answer to this question will give you information about your prospective employer and the job. You will learn what expectations the employer has for you. By phrasing the question like this, you give the interviewer the chance to picture you in the job.

Q What improvements do you want to make here, and how can I help you make them?

Phrasing this question this way allows the employer to envision you as the person she will hire. It will give you a glimpse into the job and the company's plans for the future.

Q In your opinion, how does this company compare to its major competitors, like Activate, Pump, and Dragon Works?

In preparing for the interview, you should have researched the prospective employer. When you ask this question, you are saying to the interviewer "Look at the research I've done. I know who your competitors are." The answer to this question will also help you learn more about the company.

Q From my research, I learned you sell your products both in the United States and Canada. Do you plan to expand into any other markets?

Again, you are stating something you uncovered in your research. You are also trying to learn something further about the company.

Q I know you sell hair-care products. What are the demographics of your customers?

Your reason for asking this question is similar to your reason for asking the prior one. If you have experience with the demographic this company targets, that is something you can talk about in your thank-you letter or in any follow-up interviews.

Q You mentioned that several of your clients are in the apparel business. What industries are your other clients in?

This question shows you were paying attention during the interview. You also want to learn more about the company's other clients, which demonstrates your interest in the company.

 Essential

From the interviewer's answer to one of your questions, you discover that one of your skills would be very valuable to the employer's future plans. Bring it up before you leave and again in the thank-you letter you send to follow up on the interview.

Q Never Ask: How much money will I make?

Money should never be discussed on a job interview. You should hold off on discussing salary until you receive a job offer, when you are in the right position to negotiate. Even if the employer brings it up first, it is best to avoid getting into an extensive conversation about it at this point.

Fact

Questions about religion are off limits during a job interview. An employer cannot make a decision about whether or not to hire you based on your religion. The earliest you should bring it up or ask for religious observance time is after you've accepted a job offer.

Q Never Ask: What are the health benefits like?

While you may need this information to help you decide whether or not to accept a job offer, the interview isn't the time to obtain it. Hold off on this discussion until you receive a job offer. The person interviewing you may not even know a lot about company benefits other than those she has.

Q Never Ask: How much vacation time will I have?

You haven't even started working and already you want to know about time off? Your goal during the interview is to demonstrate to the employer that you will be a productive employee. Asking about vacation time will not help you reach that goal.

Q Never Ask: Can I take time off for religious observance?

An employer is required by law to give you time off for religious observance, so you have no reason to ask about it during the interview. It should never be brought up during the interview or before you receive a job offer.

Q Never Ask: What does it take to get fired?

Asking this question is kind of like saying, "I want to do as little as possible to get by." Is that how you want the employer to see you?

CHAPTER 17

What to Do After the Interview

You spent days, maybe even weeks, getting ready for your job interview. You studied question after question, figuring out how you could best answer each one. You went through your work history to come up with anecdotes that would exemplify your ability to do the job for which you were being interviewed. Now the interview is finally over and you think you should feel relieved . . . but you don't. You haven't been offered the job yet, so all you can do is sit around and wait, right? Wrong!

Thank-You Letters

The first thing you should do after an interview, aside from submitting anything to the interviewer that he requested, is to send a thank-you letter. Many job searchers think that thank-you letters give the appearance that they are trying to "kiss up" to the interviewer. You don't have any reason to feel that way, because interviewers rarely think that. Sending a thank-you letter is a nice gesture that will let the interviewer know you appreciate the time he spent meeting with you. It will set you apart from other job candidates who choose not to send one.

Who Should Get a Thank-You Letter?

You should send a thank-you letter to each person you met with during your interview. If you had a screening interview with someone from the human resources department and then had one with a department manager, each of them should receive a thank-you note.

If someone showed you around the office, you should write a thank-you note to him as well. If you had a panel or committee interview, each person who took part should get a thank-you letter.

 Alert

Don't send letters addressed as "To Whom It May Concern." Find out the name of each person who interviewed you. If possible, write it down or get that person's business card while you're there. If you didn't manage to get someone's name, call the receptionist for that information. Ask for the correct spelling for each name—spelling counts.

What to Include

Since the primary purpose of a thank-you letter is to express your gratitude for the time the recipient spent with you, the first thing you should do is say "thank you." Next, take the opportunity to re-emphasize a skill or strength that shows you are the most qualified candidate. If you neglected to mention a particular strength that might help the interviewer make her decision, bring that up in your thank-you letter. If the interviewer voiced concern about something regarding your qualifications, this would be a good time to address that issue.

 Essential

Your thank-you letter should be short, to the point, and must never be more than one page long. It can be typed or handwritten if your writing is legible. Never address the recipient by first name. Proofread your letter carefully, and have someone else look it over too.

Finally, you should express your interest in the job by telling the interviewer you want to work for her. Let her know how she can reach you even if you have already done so. Provide your phone number and an e-mail address if you have one. You want to make it as easy as possible for her to get in touch with you.

E-Mail or Regular Mail

You may wonder whether to send your thank-you letter by e-mail or by regular mail. The problem with e-mail is that some people don't check theirs on a regular basis. Though it's hard to imagine that this is the case, it is. If you've already corresponded with the employer via e-mail, then it is perfectly okay to send a thank-you e-mail. If you haven't corresponded with her by e-mail and have never been instructed to do so, then send your letter by regular mail.

How to Format a Thank-You Letter

A thank-you letter is considered business correspondence, and you must format it accordingly. The format of your letter will differ depending on whether you are sending it by e-mail or by snail mail. In this age of electronic communication, many people have forgotten what a "hard copy" business letter even looks like. Here are the components of a business letter. Add a line after each of the following items:

- **Return address:** Your first and last name (no title) followed by your address should be the first thing on the page.
- **Date:** The date you are sending the letter should appear below the return address, with the name of the month spelled out.
- **Inside address:** The addressee's first and last name (including title, e.g., Mr., Ms., or Dr.), position, company name, and address should appear below the date. Start a new line for each of the following items: name, position, company, street address, and city/town/zip.
- **Salutation:** Your salutation should begin with "Dear" and you should always address the recipient by his title and last name (e.g., Mr. Grey), followed by a colon.
- **Body of letter:** The body of your letter should generally include an introductory paragraph that informs the reader

why you are writing to him, one or two paragraphs to give some background or supporting information, and a closing paragraph that wraps everything up and includes information about how the interviewer can reach you.

- **Closing:** End your letter with "Yours truly" or "Sincerely."
- **Signature line:** Skip four or five lines after the closing to leave enough space for your signature, and then type your full name. Don't forget to sign your name after you've printed the letter!

If you are going to send your thank-you letter by e-mail, do not place your return address at the top of the message. Instead you can include that information below your name in the "signature" section of the message. Provide your telephone number or numbers as well. There is no need to include the recipient's address or the date in your message. All e-mail messages are automatically date-stamped.

 Alert

> Do not use emoticons or e-mail shorthand in your thank-you note. Doing so will make you look unprofessional. Save those things for e-mails you send to your friends. The body of the note should follow the same guidelines as a note sent by regular mail.

Sending a thank-you letter by e-mail does not give you an excuse to be any less formal than you would be if you were sending it by regular mail. In the salutation you will address the recipient by title and last name, never by first name. You will word your letter the same way you would have if you sent it by snail mail.

Use your personal e-mail account, not a work e-mail address, to correspond with a potential employer. Do not send the e-mail from anyone's account but your own. If you share an e-mail account with your spouse, you must set up your own account for job search–related use. Use a professional-sounding e-mail address, preferably one that includes your name or initials: *ajones@cablemail.com* is good; *partygirl4eva@cablemail.com* is not.

Sample Thank-You Letters

Here are four sample thank-you letters. The first three letters are intended for the actual interviewer, and the final one is written to an administrative assistant who showed the candidate around the office. The last letter is significantly shorter than the others, and it does not make a point of reiterating any of the writer's skills, since its recipient will not be making the hiring decision and never discussed those skills with the candidate.

Sample Thank-You Letter #1

Joseph R. Green
14 Willow Street
Hoboken, NJ 07030
June 5, 2014

Ms. Maria Sanchez
Production Manager
Artistic Media
515 Madison Avenue
New York, NY 10022

Dear Ms. Sanchez:

Thank you for meeting with me this afternoon regarding the assistant production manager position at Artistic Media. I appreciate the time you spent getting to know me and explaining the specifics of the job.

I feel strongly that my experience and skills will allow me to make significant contributions to the production team. Artistic Media seems to be a company that values creativity, which is definitely one of my strengths.

I am looking forward to hearing from you within the week, as we discussed. Thank you again for your time and for considering me for this position. You can reach me by phone at (212) 555-4444 or by e-mail at *jgreene@rcat.net*.

Yours truly,
Joe Green

Sample Thank-You Letter #2

Beverly Smith
1524 South Jefferson Street
Williams, AZ 86046
September 23, 2014

Mr. Connor Shmedley
Customer Service Manager
Smart Mart Stores, Inc.
250 Adams Avenue
Flagstaff, AZ 86001

Dear Mr. Shmedley:

I appreciate your meeting with me this morning regarding the assistant customer service manager job at Smart Mart Stores. I enjoyed having the opportunity to talk to you about the improvements you have planned for the customer service department.

As I mentioned to you during the interview, before I moved to Williams, I worked at Bullseye Stores. They, as you know, have a great reputation for providing customer service. I worked closely with the department manager in implementing many of the procedures that earned Bullseye that reputation. I hope to have the opportunity to work with you to implement similar procedures at Smart Mart.

Once again, thank you for taking time out of your busy schedule today. If you have any further questions, you can reach me by phone at (520) 555-5151 or by e-mail at *bevsmith@netco.com*. I look forward to hearing your decision soon.

Sincerely,
Beverly Smith

Sample Thank-You Letter #3

Sandy Beane
37 Oak Drive
Portland, OR 97205
June 24, 2014

Dr. Pat Lee
26 Tulip Street
Portland, OR 97201

Dear Dr. Lee:

Thank you for taking time out of your busy schedule this afternoon to interview me for the office manager position. I would welcome the opportunity to work with you and the members of your staff.

As you expressed in your interview, you are looking for someone who can manage a very busy office while showing compassion for your patients. Although I have not worked in a medical office, my experience managing a law office has provided me with the skills necessary to do this job well.

Again, thank you for meeting with me. If you have additional questions, you can reach me by phone at (503) 555-1234 or by e-mail at *sbeane@horizon.net*. I look forward to hearing from you regarding your decision.

Yours truly,
Sandy Beane

Sample Thank-You Letter #4

Rose Thornton
105 Peyton Place
Chicago, IL 60637
April 17, 2014

Mr. Richard Rheinhardt
Executive Assistant
Turning Corporation
1543 48th Street
Chicago, IL 60637

Dear Mr. Rheinhardt:

I just wanted to send a quick note to thank you for showing me around your offices on Tuesday after my interview with Janet Parker.

As Ms. Parker mentioned to you, I am interviewing for the bookkeeper position. Perhaps we will get to work together.

Yours truly,
Rose Thornton

What to Do If You Don't Want the Job

After the job interview, you may decide you would not consider a job offer even if you got one. In that case, you should take yourself out of the running early. While it may be tempting to wait to find out if you got the job, it would not be proper or considerate to do so.

Even if you have decided you don't want the job after all, you should still send a thank-you letter. In that letter, you should first thank the recipient for the time she spent meeting with you. You should then say that you no longer want to be considered for the job. If you would like to explain your reasons, go ahead. This is particularly important if you want to be considered for some other position with the company in the future.

Here are two sample letters that let an interviewer know you are no longer interested in the position.

Sample Letter #1

Lisa Evans
4141 Park Road
Evanston, IL 60201
October 3, 2014

Mr. David Grand
Senior Account Executive
Triangle Corporation
314 E. Pine Street
Evanston, IL 60201

Dear Mr. Grand:

Thank you for interviewing me yesterday for the position of assistant account executive. I appreciate the time you spent with me.

After careful consideration, I have decided that I am no longer interested in this position.

Again, thank you for your time.

Yours truly,
Lisa Evans

Sample Letter #2

Thomas Jones
75 Bryant Avenue
San Francisco, CA 94108
August 6, 2014

Mr. Eric Peters
Vice President of Product Development
Q & H Corporation
402 West 3rd Street
San Francisco, CA 94108

Dear Mr. Peters:

Thank you for meeting with me yesterday afternoon regarding the marketing assistant position.

After mulling it over for the last twenty-four hours, I would like to take myself out of the running for this position. I spent three years in a similar job and feel I am now ready for a greater challenge. If a position comes up in which I can better utilize my experience and skills, I hope you'll consider me.

Thank you again for your time. If you have any questions, please call me at (415) 555-2288 or e-mail me at *tjones@homenet.com*.

Sincerely,
Tom Jones

Waiting for a Decision

After the interview, you went home and sent thank-you letters to each person you met with. Now you are sitting around waiting for the phone to ring and checking your e-mail every five minutes. Is there anything else you can do to keep yourself from going crazy while you wait to hear something?

Following Up with the Employer

While there are many situations in your life when it's okay to play hard to get, your job search isn't one of them. There are many reasons you should contact the employer to find out if he has made a decision. There aren't any reasons not to make the call.

Following up on a job interview is not only your right; it is an important strategy that should be part of your job-search campaign. A phone call to a prospective employer shows that you are not someone who is willing to sit around and wait quietly while someone else makes a decision about your future. It also gives you another opportunity to sell yourself to the employer if you find out he hasn't yet made a decision.

You may be hesitant to call an employer to find out if he has made a hiring decision because you don't want to look anxious or pushy. As long as you go about it in the right way, you won't. You should call the employer exactly one week after the interview, unless the interviewer told you he would be making a decision by a certain date. In that case, call a day after that date.

 Alert

> Don't make a pest of yourself by calling your prospective employer too often. If the employer tells you she will make a decision in a week, don't call back before then. As a general rule, don't call more than once a week. You don't want the act of finding out whether you got the job to cost you the job.

Call the person who has been your contact at the prospective employer's company. Politely, but not meekly, ask if they have made a decision yet. If they haven't, ask when they expect to make one.

The Job Offer—Finally

So, you have a job offer. Congratulations! By this time it's likely that you've decided whether you want to work for the company. Of course, you will have to consider the offer they've made and decide whether to accept it.

Negotiating a Job Offer

Some job candidates feel negotiating is a must, regardless of how good or bad that offer is. Others would not even consider negotiating and accept whatever offer they get. The truth is there is no right way to go. It all depends on the offer. It is up to you to determine if it is fair. If it isn't, you have to decide whether you want to negotiate for a better one.

If you decide to negotiate for a better offer, be sure to do your homework first. Find out how much others working in your field earn by asking around. Look at salary surveys and government data. Talk to others who work in that field. Ask other employers. Consult your trade or professional association.

 Question

Is it always possible to negotiate a job offer?
Some offers are non-negotiable. Salary and benefits may be set through a contractual arrangement between a union and an employer. If only the salary is set through such an arrangement, you may be able to negotiate other benefits, such as the amount of vacation time you will receive.

If you are looking at salary surveys or government data, you should be aware that salaries are often reported as a range. Don't compare oranges and tangerines. Candidates with more experience, greater educational levels, and better skills will lean toward the higher end of that range. You should also be aware that salaries differ according to where a job is located. Depending on regional variances in cost of living or in demand for certain skill sets, salaries can be higher in certain parts of the country. They can also vary according to your proximity to a large metropolitan area. If you get extensive benefits, such as health insurance, your monetary salary may be lower than it would be if that was not included in your offer.

A job offer isn't official until you see it in black and white. Do not give notice to your current employer until you have a written offer from your future one. You should, in turn, send a written acceptance of the offer. If you decide to decline the offer, it is polite to send the employer a letter to let her know. Good luck with your new job!

Resources

Websites

The Internet is a great place to turn for career-related information. You can get career and job search advice, find job listings, and research occupations, salaries, and prospective employers.

Career and Job Search Advice Websites

ABOUT.COM CAREER PLANNING

The Everything® Job Interview Question Book author Dawn Rosenberg McKay's site covers all aspects of career planning, including career choice, job hunting, job training, legal issues, and the workplace.

careerplanning.about.com

ABOUT.COM JOB SEARCHING

Alison Doyle, the guide to this excellent site, helps you with all aspects of online job searching, writing resumes and cover letters, references, interviewing skills, and unemployment.

jobsearch.about.com

MONSTER CAREER ADVICE

Find resume and job interviewing tips, salary information, relocating advice, and diversity advice from Monster.com.

content.monster.com

RILEY GUIDE

Librarian Margaret F. Dikel has organized myriad sites that can help you with your job search.

www.rileyguide.com

Online Job Banks

CAREERBUILDER.COM
Search for jobs in the United States and internationally by company or title. Post your resume and CareerBuilder will give you job recommendations.
www.careerbuilder.com

GOVTJOBS.COM
Search for jobs within states, counties, towns, and cities.
www.govtjobs.com

INDEED
Indeed is a job search engine. When you put in your search criteria, it looks through many different sites, including job boards, corporate websites, professional association websites, and newspapers.
www.indeed.com

MONSTER
Search for jobs by location or job category. You can also enter keywords to search by job titles, company names, and requirements. Post your resume online so employers can find you. You can even ask Monster to send you an e-mail when new jobs match your search.
www.monster.com

SIMPLYHIRED
Go to this site to find job listings gathered from company websites, classified ads, and job boards.
www.simplyhired.com

USAJOBS
This is the official site of the U.S. Office of Personnel Management. You can search for jobs with the federal government, create a resume, and download related forms.
www.usajobs.com

Company Research Resources and Tools

BLOGLINES
A web-based newsfeed reader that allows you to subscribe to and read newsfeeds and blogs.
bloglines.com

GOOGLE BLOG SEARCH
Locate blogs about the industries and companies you are researching.
blogsearch.google.com

PR NEWSWIRE
Use this site to search for press releases put out by various companies.
prnewswire.com

SECURITY AND EXCHANGE COMMISSION FILINGS AND FORMS (EDGAR)

The Securities and Exchange Commission requires publicly held companies to file information about finances each quarter and information about material events or corporate changes as they occur. You can retrieve this information from the EDGAR database.
sec.gov/edgar.shtml

TECHNORATI BLOG SEARCH

Use this site to search for blogs that cover a particular industry or company. You can also search for individual blog posts by topic.
technorati.com

Occupation and Salary Information

JOBSTAR PROFESSION-SPECIFIC SALARY SURVEYS

Look here for salary information for dozens of occupations.
jobstar.org/tools/salary/sal-prof.cfm

WORKING IN CANADA

This resource contains descriptions of occupations and labor market information. The Canadian government produces it. You will find information for the country and individual provinces and cities.
www.workingincanada.gc.ca

OCCUPATIONAL OUTLOOK HANDBOOK

Use this resource, published by the U.S. Bureau of Labor Statistics and updated biannually, to get job descriptions. Learn about working conditions, training and education needed, employment outlook, salary, and expected job prospects for a wide number of occupations. Information is also available in Spanish.
www.bls.gov/ooh

SALARY.COM

Get salary information for a variety of occupations. Search by job title and location for salaries in the U.S. You can also find information for Canada.
www.salary.com

Career Networking

FACEBOOK

Although it is usually used for social networking, Facebook can also be used to network with other professionals.
www.facebook.com

LINKEDIN
Use this online network to connect with other professionals, search for jobs, and get found by potential employers.
www.linkedin.com

Miscellaneous Sites

ACTION WORDS FROM PURDUE UNIVERSITY'S ONLINE WRITING LAB
Are you looking for just the right word to describe your skills and accomplishments? You will find it here, arranged into categories.
owl.english.purdue.edu/owl/resource/543/02

EQUAL EMPLOYMENT OPPORTUNITY COMMISSION
This government agency was established by the Civil Rights Act of 1964 and protects U.S. workers from many types of employment discrimination. The EEOC website has information on all the laws the agency enforces and advice on how to file a claim.
www.eeoc.gov

EXECUTIVEPLANET.COM
This website includes business culture guides for international businesspeople.
www.executiveplanet.com

Books

Job Search Advice
Bolles, Richard Nelson. *What Color Is Your Parachute: A Practical Manual for Job-Hunters and Career-Changers.* Berkeley, CA: Ten Speed Press, Annual.

Doyle, Alison. *Internet Your Way to a New Job, 3rd Edition.* Happy About, 2011.

McKay, Dawn Rosenberg. *The Everything® Get-a-Job Book, 2nd Edition.* Avon, MA: Adams Media, 2007.

Yate, Martin. *Knock 'em Dead: The Ultimate Job Search Guide.* Avon, MA: Adams Media, Annual.

Career Advancement
Covey, Stephen R. *The 7 Habits of Highly Effective People, Revised Edition.* New York: Free Press, 2009.

Darling, Diane. *The Networking Survival Guide, 2nd Edition.* New York: McGraw-Hill, 2010.

Cover Letters and Resumes

Enelow, Wendy S., and Louise M. Kursmark. *Expert Resumes for Computer and Web Jobs, 3rd Edition.* St. Paul, MN: JIST Publishing, 2011.

————. *Expert Resumes for Health Care Careers, 2nd Edition.* St. Paul, MN: JIST Publishing, 2010.

————. *Expert Resumes for People Returning to Work.* St. Paul, MN: JIST Publishing, 2007.

Kursmark, Louise M. *Best Resumes for College Students and New Grads, 3rd Edition.* St. Paul, MN: JIST Publishing, 2011.

Noble, David F. *Gallery of Best Resumes for People without a Four-Year Degree, 4th Edition.* St. Paul, MN: JIST Publishing, 2009.

Parker, Yana. *The Damn Good Resume Guide: A Crash Course in Resume Writing, 5th Edition.* Berkeley, CA: Ten Speed Press, 2012.

————. *The Resume Catalog: 200 Damn Good Examples.* Berkeley, CA: Ten Speed Press, 1996.

Wallace, Richard. *Adams Cover Letter Almanac, 2nd Edition.* Avon, MA: Adams Media, 2006.

————. *Adams Resume Almanac, 2nd Edition.* Avon, MA: Adams Media, 2005.

Yate, Martin. *Knock 'em Dead Cover Letters, 10th Edition.* Avon, MA: Adams Media, 2012.

————. *Knock 'em Dead Resumes, 10th Edition.* Avon, MA: Adams Media, 2012.

Interview Etiquette

Post, Emily, and Peter Post. *Emily Post's The Etiquette Advantage in Business.* New York: HarperCollins, 2005.

Sabath, Ann Marie. *Business Etiquette: 101 Ways to Conduct Business with Charm and Savvy, 3rd Edition.* Pompton Plains, NJ: Career Press, 2010.

International Job Searching

Axtell, Roger E. *Essential Do's and Taboos: The Complete Guide to International Business and Leisure Travel.* Hoboken, NJ: John Wiley & Sons, 2007.

Krannich, Ronald L., and Wendy S. Enelow. *Best Resumes and CVs for International Jobs: Your Passport to the Global Job Market.* Manassas Park, VA: Impact Publications, 2002.

Morrison, Terri. *Kiss, Bow, or Shake Hands, 2nd Edition:*

The Bestselling Guide to Doing Business in More Than 60 Countries. Avon, MA: Adams Media, 2006.

Salary Negotiation

Chapman, Jack. *Negotiating Your Salary: How to Make $1000 a Minute, 7th Edition.* Berkeley, CA: Ten Speed Press, 2011.

Hopkinson, Jim. *Salary Tutor: Learn the Salary Negotiation Secrets No One Ever Taught You.* Business Plus, 2011.

Index

254

We Have EVERYTHING® on Anything!

With more than 19 million copies sold, the Everything® series has become one of America's favorite resources for solving problems, learning new skills, and organizing lives. Our brand is not only recognizable—it's also welcomed.

The series is a hand-in-hand partner for people who are ready to tackle new subjects—like you!

For more information on the Everything® series, please visit *www.adamsmedia.com*.

The Everything® list spans a wide range of subjects, with more than 500 titles covering 25 different categories:

Business	History	Reference
Careers	Home Improvement	Religion
Children's Storybooks	Everything Kids	Self-Help
Computers	Languages	Sports & Fitness
Cooking	Music	Travel
Crafts and Hobbies	New Age	Wedding
Education/Schools	Parenting	Writing
Games and Puzzles	Personal Finance	
Health	Pets	